It's another Quality Book from CGP

This book has been carefully written for
children working towards a Level 4.

It matches the Attainment Targets perfectly.

It contains lots of questions on the Maths you should
know to get a Level 4 — because practice is
the only way you'll get any better.

It's also got some practice tests so you can
see if you really know your stuff.

What CGP is all about

Our sole aim here at CGP is to produce the highest quality
books — carefully written, immaculately presented and
dangerously close to being funny.

Then we work our socks off to get them out to you
— at the cheapest possible prices.

Contents

SECTION ONE — COUNTING AND UNDERSTANDING NUMBER

SECTION TWO — KNOWING AND USING NUMBER FACTS

SECTION THREE — CALCULATING

SECTION FOUR — UNDERSTANDING SHAPE

SECTION FIVE — MEASURING

SECTION SIX — HANDLING DATA

SECTION SEVEN — USING AND APPLYING MATHEMATICS

Published by Coordination Group Publications Ltd.

Editors:
Joe Brazier, Charley Darbishire, Heather Gregson, Luke von Kotze, Simon Little,
Michael Southorn, Sarah Williams.

Contributor:
Simon Greaves

ISBN: 978 1 84762 198 6

With thanks to Glenn Rogers, Tina Ramsden and Isabelle Darbishire for the proofreading.
Also thanks to Jan Greenway for the copyright research and John Cullen for the content review.

Thumb illustration used throughout the book © iStockphoto.com.

Groovy website: www.cgpbooks.co.uk

Printed by Elanders Hindson Ltd, Newcastle upon Tyne.
Jolly bits of clipart from CorelDRAW®

About the Book

This Book is Full of Level 4 Maths Questions

There are questions on all the important Level 4 topics.

They are like SATs questions so they're <u>good practice</u>.

This book also has <u>four practice tests</u>.

There's a 'difficult' Level 3 test, two 'easy' Level 4 tests, and one 'difficult' Level 4 test.

> This book covers all the <u>Attainment Targets</u> for Level 4. They say what children working at Level 4 can usually do.

This Book Matches our Level 4 Study Book

The Level 4 Study Book can help you if you get <u>stuck</u>.

It explains all the maths you should know to get a Level 4.

At the <u>back of this book</u> are

answers to all of the questions.

I wonder if the answers are in here.

There are Learning Objectives on All Pages

Learning Objectives say <u>what you need to know</u>.

Use the <u>tick circles</u> to show how well you understand the maths.

Use a pencil. You can <u>tick other circles</u> as you get better.

I can win silver at the Olympics.

Tick here if you can do some of the Learning Objective.

If you're struggling, tick here.

Tick this circle if you can do the Learning Objective really well.

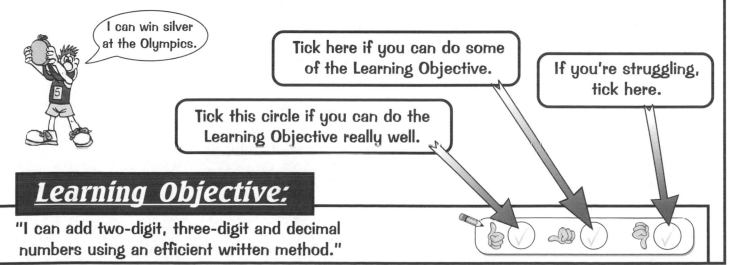

Learning Objective:

"I can add two-digit, three-digit and decimal numbers using an efficient written method."

Practice Test 1 — Levels 3B and 3A

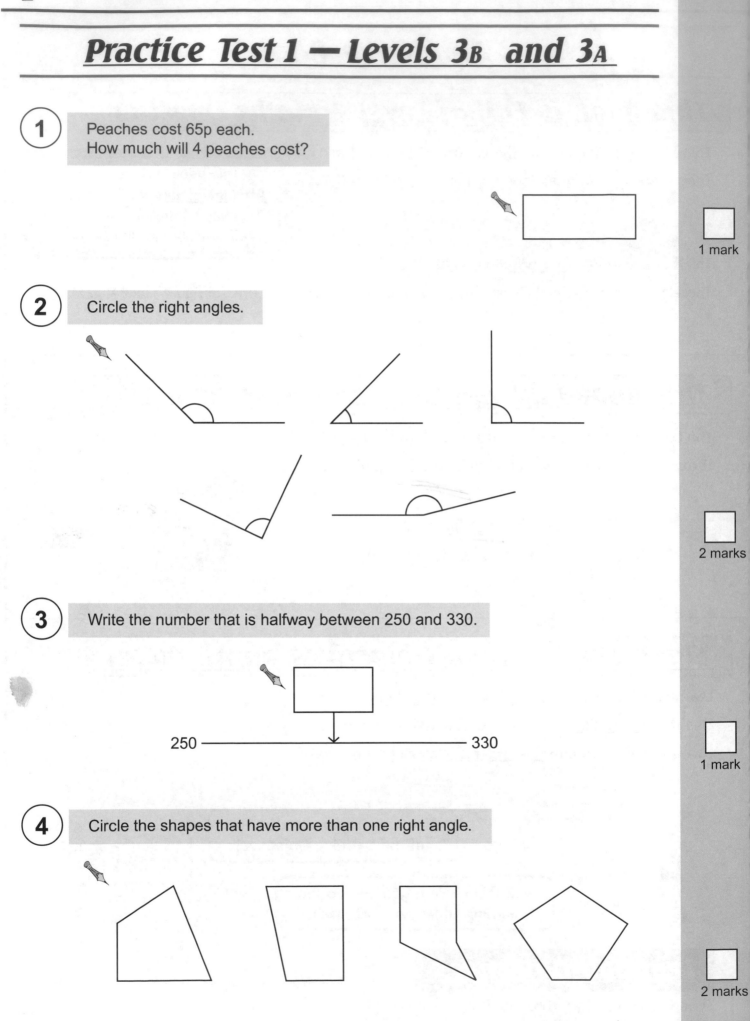

1 Peaches cost 65p each.
How much will 4 peaches cost?

1 mark

2 Circle the right angles.

2 marks

3 Write the number that is halfway between 250 and 330.

250 ——————————————— 330

1 mark

4 Circle the shapes that have more than one right angle.

2 marks

5 What is the remainder when 34 is divided by 6?

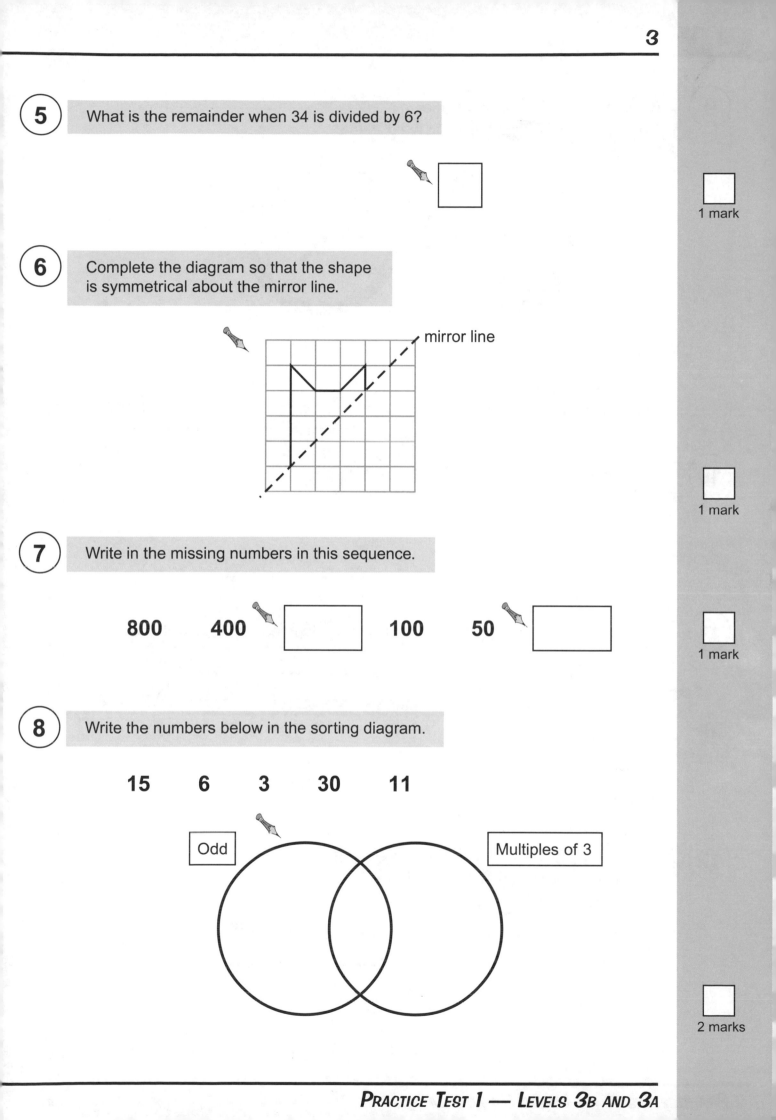

1 mark

6 Complete the diagram so that the shape is symmetrical about the mirror line.

mirror line

1 mark

7 Write in the missing numbers in this sequence.

800   400   100   50

1 mark

8 Write the numbers below in the sorting diagram.

15   6   3   30   11

Odd   Multiples of 3

2 marks

4

9 These clocks show the time that a train left a station and the time it arrived at the next one.

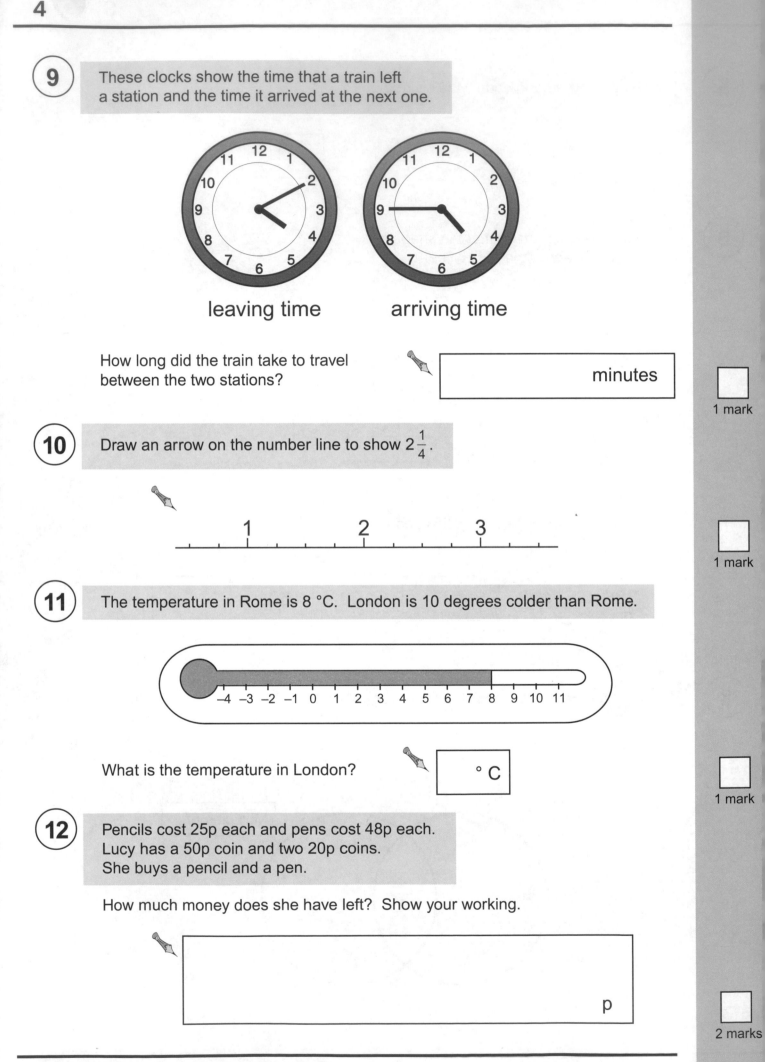

leaving time   arriving time

How long did the train take to travel between the two stations?

| minutes |

1 mark

10 Draw an arrow on the number line to show $2\frac{1}{4}$.

1   2   3

1 mark

11 The temperature in Rome is 8 °C. London is 10 degrees colder than Rome.

−4 −3 −2 −1 0 1 2 3 4 5 6 7 8 9 10 11

What is the temperature in London?

| ° C |

1 mark

12 Pencils cost 25p each and pens cost 48p each.
Lucy has a 50p coin and two 20p coins.
She buys a pencil and a pen.

How much money does she have left? Show your working.

p

2 marks

13 Ian collected information about hair colour in his class.
He wrote his results in the table shown.

The graph below shows the information
from the table. Fill in the empty boxes.

Hair colour	Number of children
Brown	5
Black	10
Blond	3
Red	7

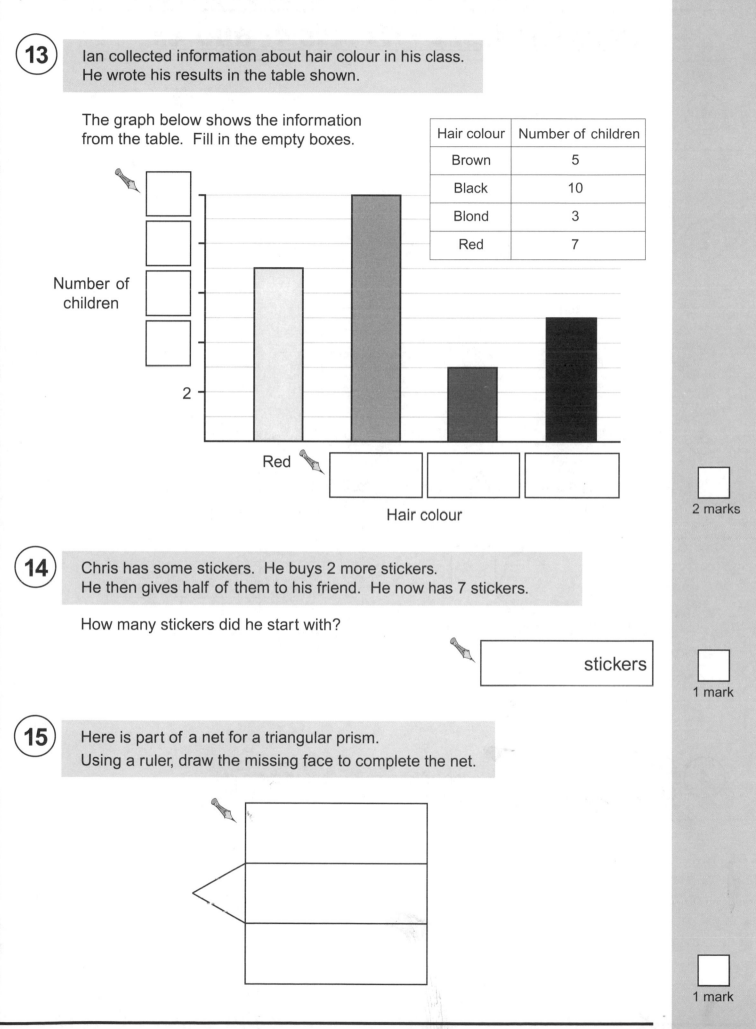

Number of children

2

Red

Hair colour

2 marks

14 Chris has some stickers. He buys 2 more stickers.
He then gives half of them to his friend. He now has 7 stickers.

How many stickers did he start with?

stickers

1 mark

15 Here is part of a net for a triangular prism.
Using a ruler, draw the missing face to complete the net.

1 mark

Practice Test 2 — Levels 4c and 4b

1 Complete this addition.

759 + 468 = [   ]

2 Ben watches a film. It starts at 12:25 and finishes at 14:50.
How long was the film?

| hours   minutes |

3 The table shows the number of goals scored by five netball teams.

What is the mode value of the
goals scored?

[   ]

What is the range of values?

[   ]

Team	Number of goals
A	5
B	4
C	5
D	2
E	3

4 Adrian has drawn these four nets for a square-based pyramid.
Circle the nets that are correct.

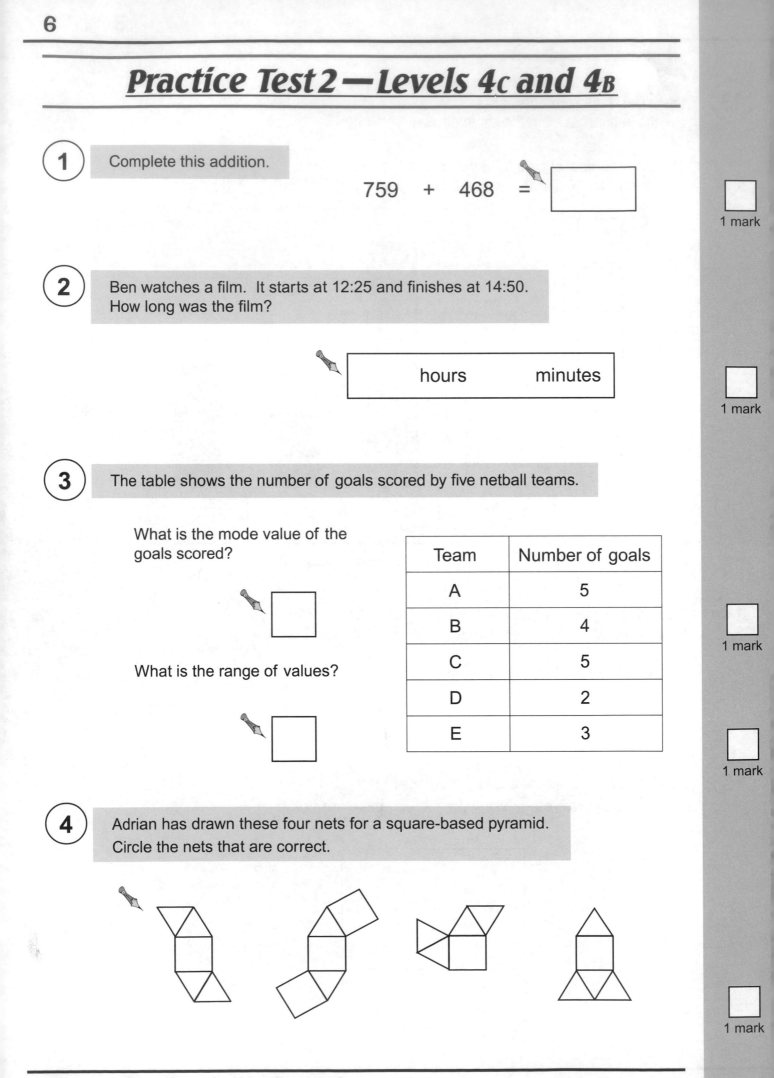

5 Write the largest and the smallest whole numbers you can make using all of the digits below.

2   8   7   5

largest	smallest

largest   smallest

1 mark

6 Circle the shapes that have an area of 6 squares.

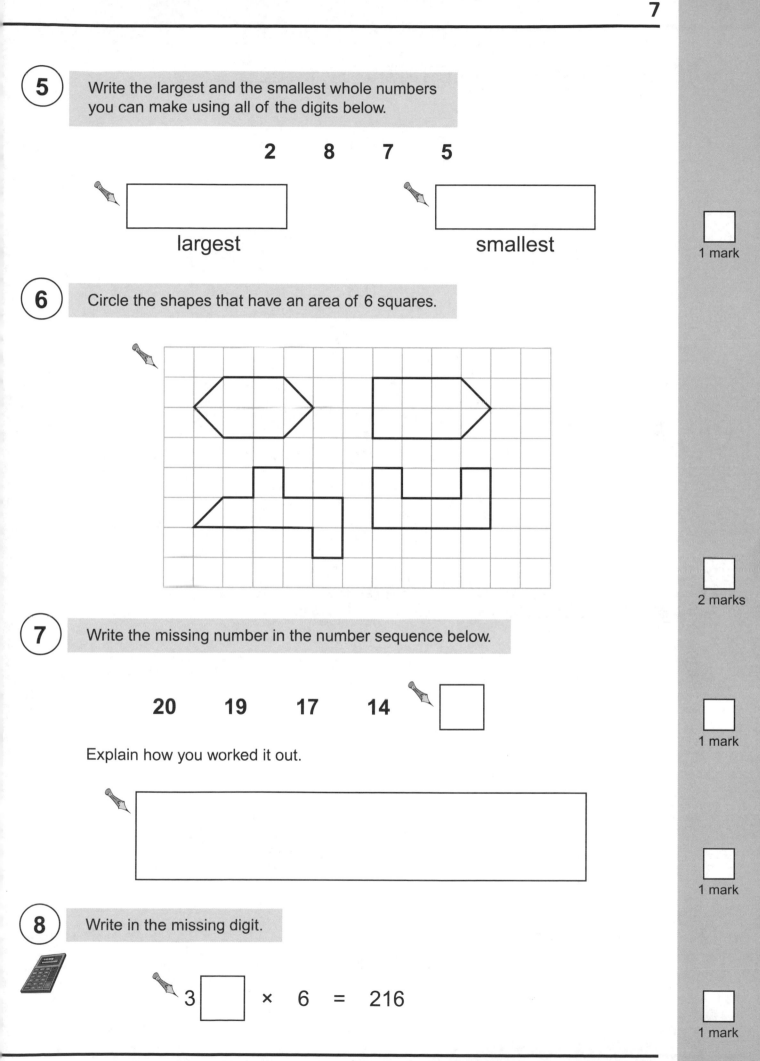

2 marks

7 Write the missing number in the number sequence below.

20   19   17   14

Explain how you worked it out.

1 mark

1 mark

8 Write in the missing digit.

3 ☐ × 6 = 216

1 mark

9 Draw lines to join the fractions and decimals that have the same value.

$\frac{2}{5}$

$\frac{3}{4}$

$\frac{7}{10}$

0.4

0.75

0.7

0.3

0.25

1 mark

10 Find $\frac{1}{3}$ of 36.

1 mark

11 Jo has made a pattern with some triangular tiles on her wall.
The tiles are all equilateral triangles.

What is the perimeter of the shape Jo has made?

cm

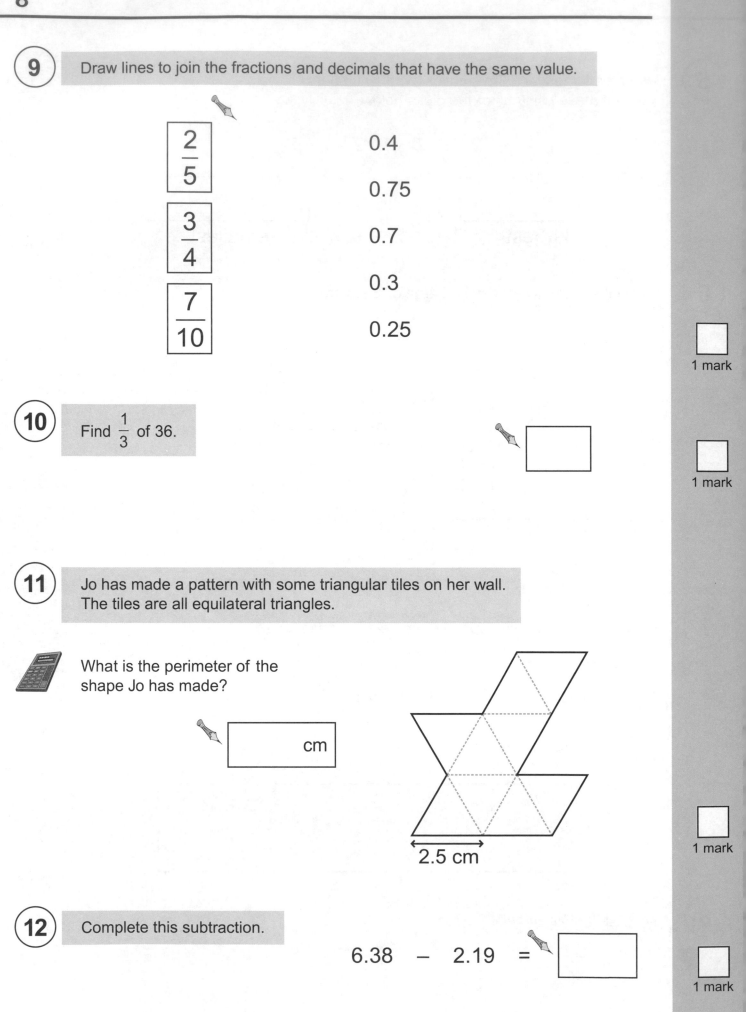

2.5 cm

1 mark

12 Complete this subtraction.

6.38 − 2.19 =

1 mark

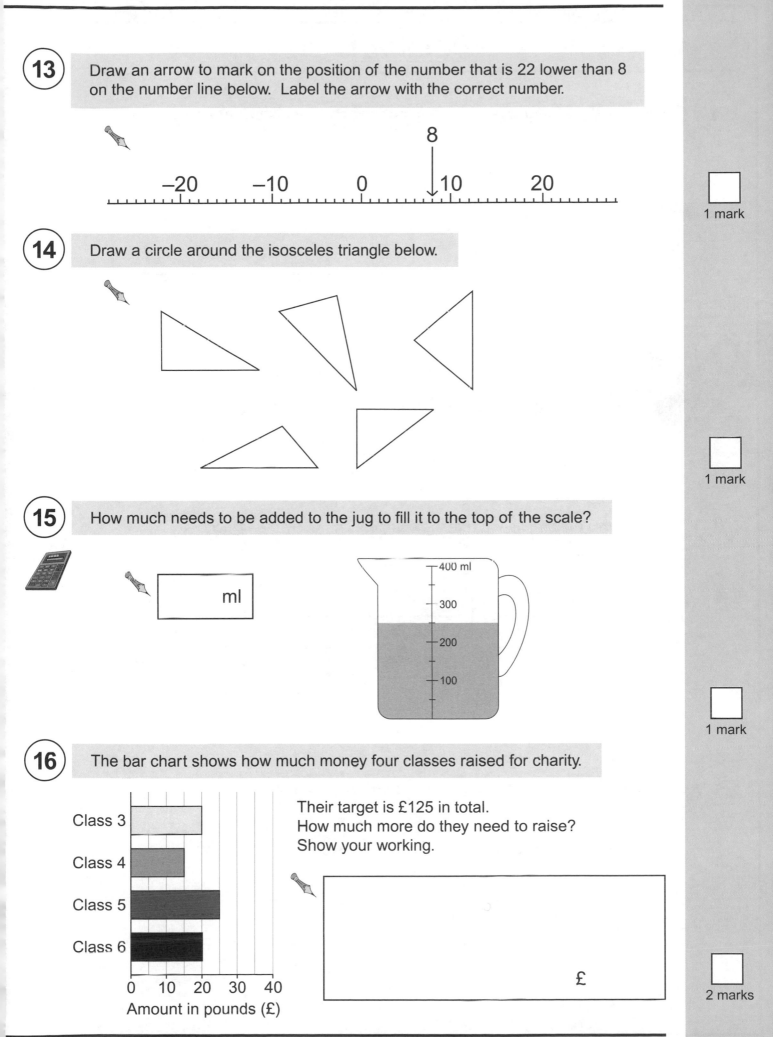

Decimals

1 Partition 25.351 into tens, units, tenths, hundredths and thousandths.

1 mark

2 Circle the smallest number below.

0.460   **0.64**   **0.046**   **0.064**   **6.04**

1 mark

3 Look at this number line. Write the numbers shown by the arrows.

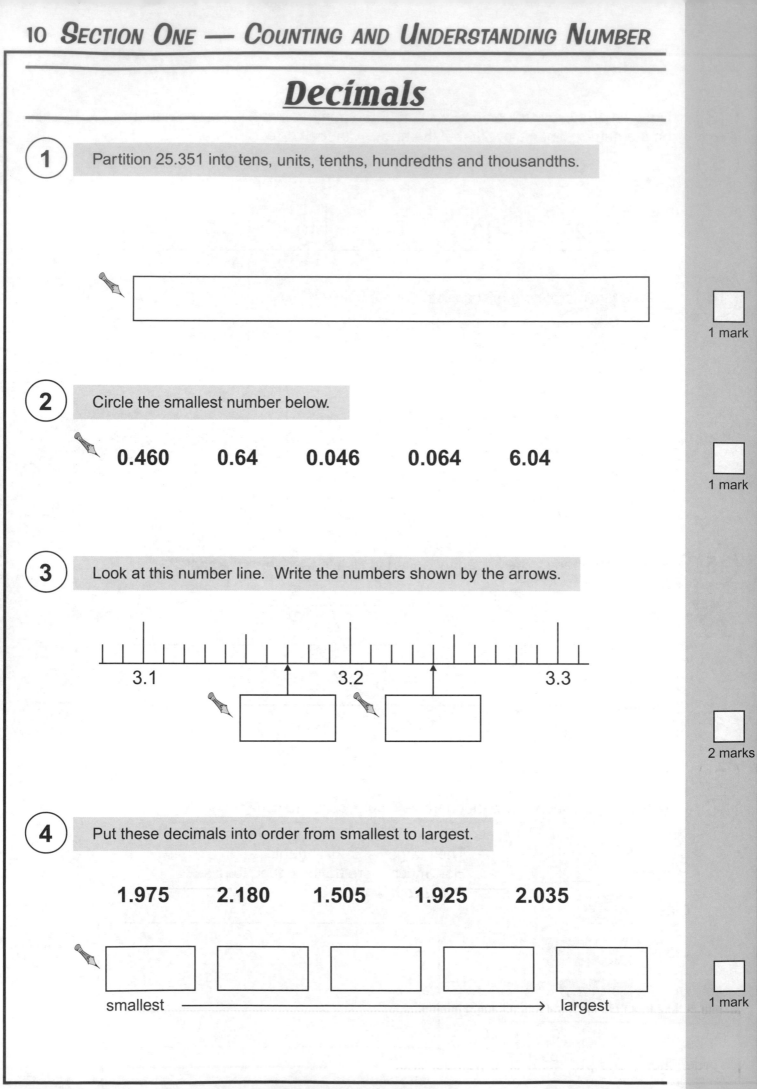

3.1   3.2   3.3

2 marks

4 Put these decimals into order from smallest to largest.

1.975   2.180   1.505   1.925   2.035

smallest ———————————————→ largest

1 mark

Decimals

(5) Circle the number which is closest to 1.

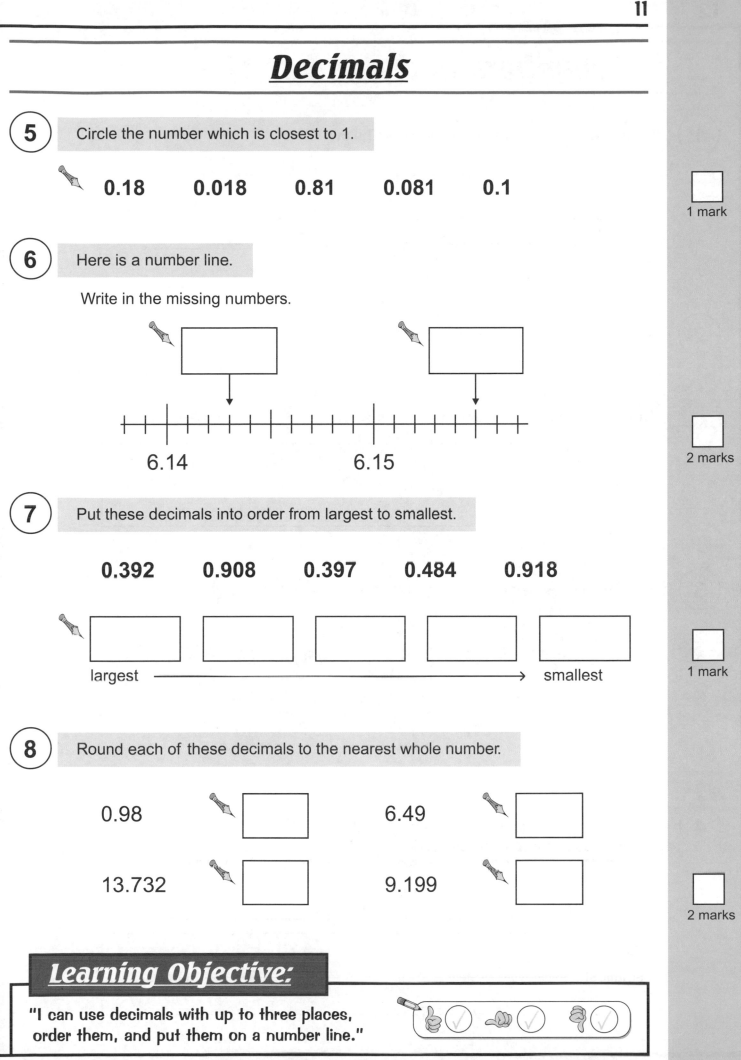

0.18   **0.018**   **0.81**   **0.081**   **0.1**

1 mark

(6) Here is a number line.

Write in the missing numbers.

6.14   6.15

2 marks

(7) Put these decimals into order from largest to smallest.

0.392   **0.908**   **0.397**   **0.484**   **0.918**

largest ————————————————————→ smallest

1 mark

(8) Round each of these decimals to the nearest whole number.

0.98   6.49

13.732   9.199

2 marks

Learning Objective:

"I can use decimals with up to three places,
order them, and put them on a number line."

Numbers and Number Lines

1 Write the missing numbers in the boxes below.

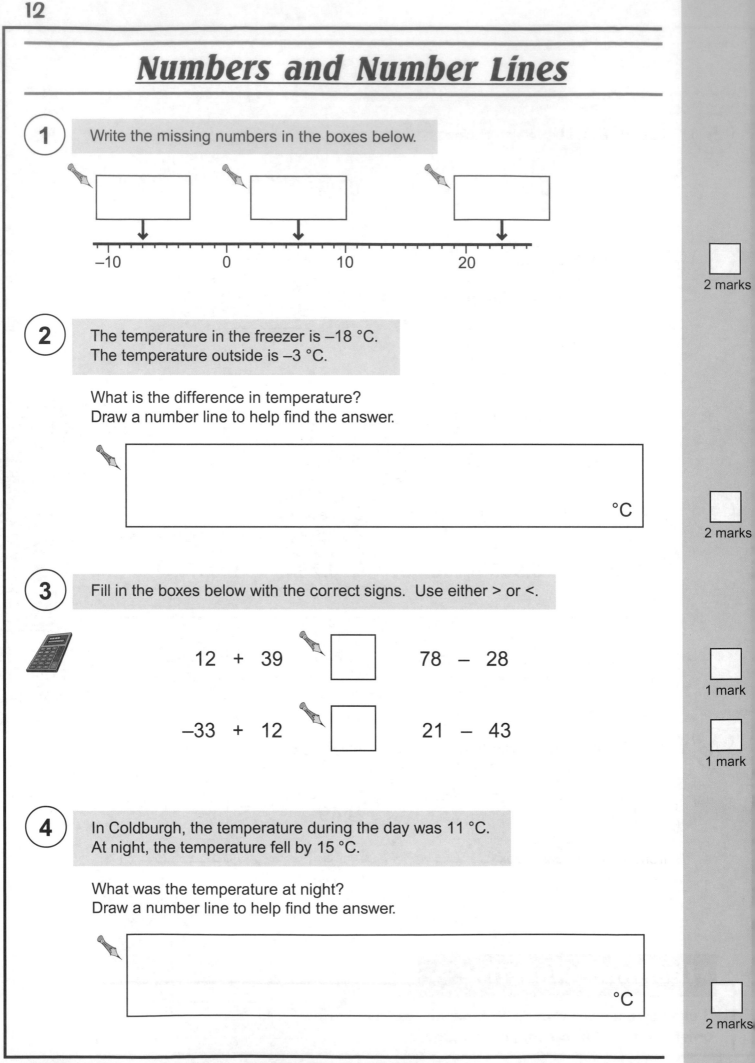

-10   0   10   20

2 marks

2 The temperature in the freezer is –18 °C.
The temperature outside is –3 °C.

What is the difference in temperature?
Draw a number line to help find the answer.

°C

2 marks

3 Fill in the boxes below with the correct signs. Use either > or <.

12 + 39   ☐   78 – 28

1 mark

–33 + 12   ☐   21 – 43

1 mark

4 In Coldburgh, the temperature during the day was 11 °C.
At night, the temperature fell by 15 °C.

What was the temperature at night?
Draw a number line to help find the answer.

°C

2 marks

SECTION ONE — COUNTING AND UNDERSTANDING NUMBER

Numbers and Number Lines

5 Sea level is at 0 m, the top of a mountain is at 1300 m and the bottom of the sea is at –2800 m.

Draw lines to mark their positions on the number line.
The first one has been done for you.

| sea level | | sea bottom | | mountain top |

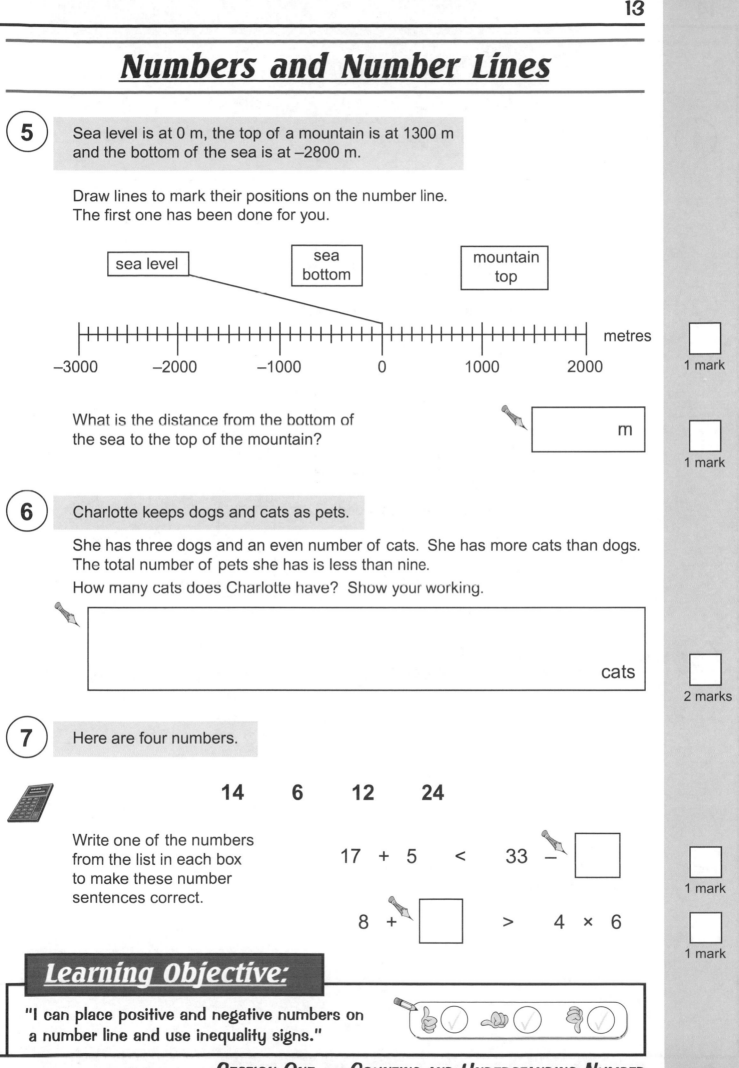

metres

−3000   −2000   −1000   0   1000   2000

☐ 1 mark

What is the distance from the bottom of the sea to the top of the mountain?

☐ m

☐ 1 mark

6 Charlotte keeps dogs and cats as pets.

She has three dogs and an even number of cats. She has more cats than dogs.
The total number of pets she has is less than nine.
How many cats does Charlotte have? Show your working.

cats

☐ 2 marks

7 Here are four numbers.

14   6   12   24

Write one of the numbers from the list in each box to make these number sentences correct.

17 + 5   <   33 − ☐

☐ 1 mark

8 + ☐   >   4 × 6

☐ 1 mark

Learning Objective:

"I can place positive and negative numbers on a number line and use inequality signs."

👍 ✓   👌 ✓   👎 ✓

SECTION ONE — COUNTING AND UNDERSTANDING NUMBER

Percentages

1 Write these fractions as percentages.

$\frac{85}{100}$ 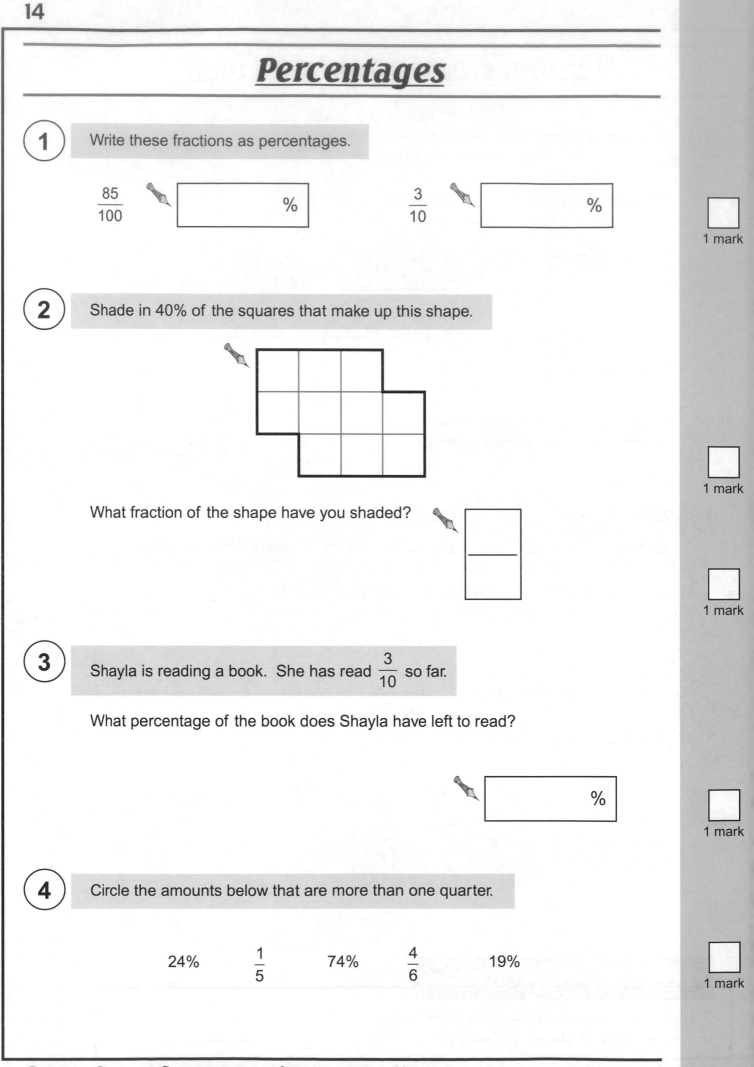 [ ] %

$\frac{3}{10}$ [ ] %

1 mark

2 Shade in 40% of the squares that make up this shape.

What fraction of the shape have you shaded? [ ]

1 mark

1 mark

3 Shayla is reading a book. She has read $\frac{3}{10}$ so far.

What percentage of the book does Shayla have left to read?

[ ] %

1 mark

4 Circle the amounts below that are more than one quarter.

24% $\frac{1}{5}$ 74% $\frac{4}{6}$ 19%

1 mark

Percentages

5 Circle the amount of each shape that is shaded.

The first one has been done for you.

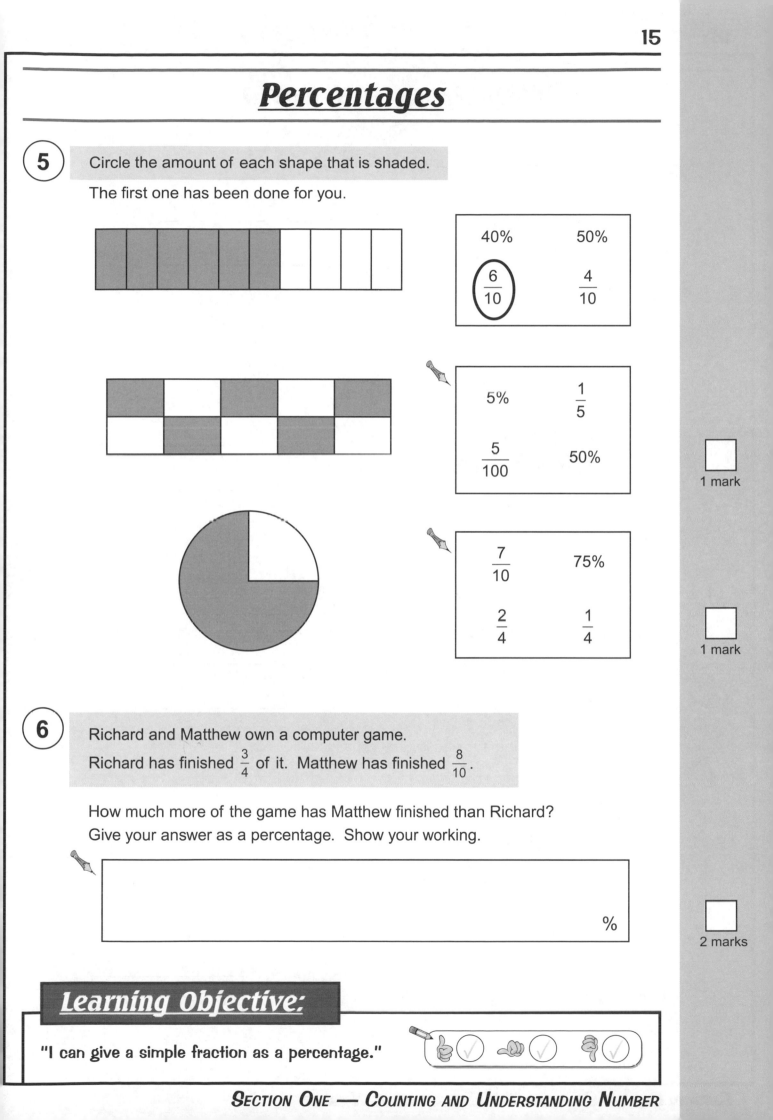

40%	50%
$\boxed{\frac{6}{10}}$	$\frac{4}{10}$

5%	$\frac{1}{5}$
$\frac{5}{100}$	50%

1 mark

$\frac{7}{10}$	75%
$\frac{2}{4}$	$\frac{1}{4}$

1 mark

6 Richard and Matthew own a computer game.

Richard has finished $\frac{3}{4}$ of it. Matthew has finished $\frac{8}{10}$.

How much more of the game has Matthew finished than Richard?
Give your answer as a percentage. Show your working.

%

2 marks

Learning Objective:

"I can give a simple fraction as a percentage."

SECTION ONE — COUNTING AND UNDERSTANDING NUMBER

Proportion and Ratio

1 A doughnut costs 35p. How much will 5 doughnuts cost?

£ _____

1 mark

35p

2 A bag of 4 cookies costs £1.80. How much does 1 cookie cost?

_____ p

1 mark

£1.80

3 Jill can swim one length of a pool every half a minute.

She swims for $3\frac{1}{2}$ minutes without stopping. How many lengths does she swim?

_____ lengths

1 mark

4 Sanjay saves £6 every week.

After two weeks he has saved £12.

Weeks   0   1   2   3   4   5   6   7   8   9   10

£   0   6   12

How much will Sanjay have saved after seven weeks?   £ _____

1 mark

Proportion and Ratio

5 There are 32 pupils in a class. They are divided equally into 8 teams.

How many pupils are there in 5 teams? Show your working.

| |
| |
| pupils |

2 marks

6 James and Mila are having roast dinner.

James has 6 potatoes. He has 3 carrots for every 2 potatoes.
How many carrots does he have?

| carrots |

1 mark

Mila has 4 potatoes. For every 2 potatoes, she has 7 green beans.
How many green beans does Mila have?

| green beans |

1 mark

7 On a farm, there are 7 chickens for every 2 pigs.

There are 42 chickens. How many pigs are there? Show your working.

| |
| |
| pigs |

2 marks

8 Robin has 54 eggs and some boxes.

He puts the same number of eggs into each box.
4 boxes contain 24 eggs in total. How many boxes are there altogether?
Show your working.

| |
| |
| boxes |

2 marks

Learning Objective:

"I can use the relationships between numbers
to solve ratio and proportion questions."

Checking Calculations

1 The answer to a sum is 430 when rounded to the nearest 10.

The actual answer is a whole number.

What is the smallest number the actual answer could be?

1 mark

What is the biggest number the actual answer could be?

1 mark

2 Raj subtracts 19 from a number. His answer is 24.

What number did Raj start with?

1 mark

3 Jim calculates that 2032 − 794 = 1238.

Write an addition you could use to check Jim's calculation.
Is he right? Write YES or NO.

1 mark

4 Lucy divides 144 sweets equally between 9 bags.

Lucy says, "There are 6 sweets in each bag."
Explain how you know that Lucy is probably wrong without doing the calculation.

1 mark

Checking Calculations

5 Write two calculations you could do to check 91 ÷ 7 = 13.

1 mark

1 mark

6 Estimate 7.2 minus 2.9 by rounding to the nearest whole number.

1 mark

7 Circle the best estimate of the value of 12.3 × 9.8.

108   100   120   130

1 mark

8 Look at the menu.

Menu

Sandwiches:	Ham	£2.49
	Cheese	£2.22
	Tuna	£2.33
	Chicken	£3.12
Soups:	Tomato	£1.13
	Onion	£1.07
Drinks:	Coffee	£1.27
	Tea	£1.05
	Cans	78p
Crisps:		51p

Greg wants to buy a cheese sandwich, a cup of tea and a packet of crisps. Estimate the total cost by rounding each price to the nearest 50p.

1 mark

Is this estimate higher or lower than the actual cost?

1 mark

Learning Objective:

"I can check the result of a calculation."

Factors and Multiples

1 Here is a repeating number and shape pattern. The pattern carries on for ever.

▽1 ◯2 ▽3 ◯4 ▽5 ◯6 ▽7 ◯8

Decide whether these statements are true or false. Circle the correct answer.

15 will be in a circle. True False

1 mark

All numbers in circles are multiples of two. True False

1 mark

Ria says, "Every square number will be in a circle."
Explain why Ria is not correct.

1 mark

2 Look at these four digit cards. 4 7 3 2

Use two of the cards to make a two-digit number which is:

a multiple of 6

1 mark

a factor of 54

1 mark

3 Circle all the multiples of 4 on this list.

16   22   24   27   29

1 mark

4 Write down all the factor pairs of 32.

1 mark

Factors and Multiples

5 Put a number less than 30 in each section of the table.

	multiple of 7	not a multiple of 7
even		
not even		

2 marks

6 Becky says all multiples of 8 end in 2, 4, 6 or 8.

Is Becky right? Circle: YES or NO.

Give an example to show how you know.

1 mark

7 Find a common multiple of 6 and 8.

1 mark

8 Look at this number sequence.

Fill in the next two numbers.

1,   5,   9,   13,   17,   ☐ , ☐

1 mark

Will 84 be part of the sequence? Circle: YES or NO.
Explain your answer.

1 mark

Learning Objective:

"I can find pairs of factors that multiply to make a given number. I can find a common multiple of two numbers."

Multiplication and Division

1 Circle two numbers that multiply together to give an answer of 21.

6   3   2   7   11

1 mark

2 Circle all the multiples of 9 in this list:

27   19   36   54   43

1 mark

3 Vera writes down the multiplication 7 × 4 = 28.

Use the same three numbers to write another multiplication and a division.

[   ] × [   ] = [   ]

[   ] ÷ [   ] = [   ]

1 mark

4 Work out:

Twenty-eight divided by seven   [   ]

1 mark

Forty multiplied by eight   [   ]

1 mark

Fifty-four divided by nine   [   ]

1 mark

Multiplication and Division

5 Here are four digit cards.

| 6 | 7 | 4 | 2 |

Use two of the digits to make:

a multiple of 9

a multiple of 8

1 mark

1 mark

6 Jane thinks of a number. She divides it by six and adds two.

She gets an answer of 9. What number was she thinking of?

1 mark

7 Six-packs of cereal are on special offer. Each pack has an extra cereal box free.

CEREAL | 6 BOXES + 1 FREE | CEREAL

Derek wants to get 56 boxes of cereal in total.
How many packs should Derek buy?

packs

1 mark

8 Lesley has 84 sweets. She shares them out between her friends.

Each friend gets nine sweets. There are three sweets left over.
How many friends are the sweets shared between?

1 mark

Learning Objective:

"I know my times tables to 10 × 10."

Square Numbers

(1) What is seven squared?

1 mark

(2) Monique says: "The only square number that's a multiple of 4 is 16."

Is Monique's statement true or false?

Circle the correct answer: TRUE   FALSE

Give an example to explain your answer.

1 mark

(3) Use the answer to 6 × 6 to help you find 60 × 60.

2 marks

(4) Put a number under 30 in each section of the table.

	square number	not a square number
multiple of 3		
not a multiple of 3		

2 marks

Square Numbers

5 Write down the next square number after 16.

1 mark

6 Here is a list of numbers. Circle the square numbers.

25   39   45   64   72   121

1 mark

7 Are there any square numbers between 70 and 80?

Circle: YES   or   NO.
Explain how you know.

1 mark

1 mark

8 Answer these questions:

Which two square numbers add together to make 10?

[ ] and [ ]

1 mark

Which two square numbers add together to make 25?

[ ] and [ ]

1 mark

Learning Objective:

"I can say the squares of numbers to 12 × 12 and work out the squares of multiples of 10."

SECTION TWO — KNOWING AND USING NUMBER FACTS

Multiply and Divide by 10 and 100

1 Multiply seventy-five by one hundred.

1 mark

2 What is one hundred and sixty divided by ten?

1 mark

3 Write in the missing number.

$$5300 \div \boxed{} = 100$$

1 mark

4 How many 1 pence coins would I need to buy the following items?

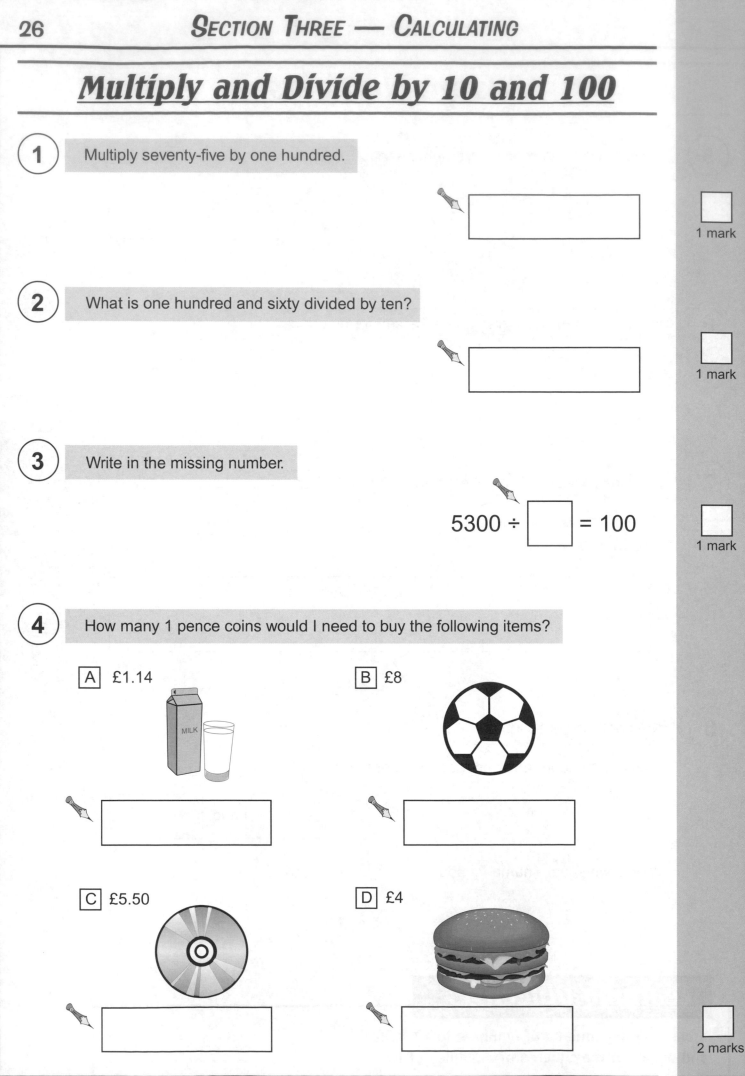

A £1.14

B £8

C £5.50

D £4

2 marks

Multiply and Divide by 10 and 100

5 Multiply forty-five point three by ten.

1 mark

6 Write in the missing number.

$$4.6 \times \boxed{} = 460$$

1 mark

7 What is eight hundred and sixty-three divided by one hundred?

1 mark

8 Look at these presents.

| A | £1.20 | B | £12 | C | £120 | D | £1200 |

Write the letter of the present that costs:

One hundred times more than £1.20

Ten times more than £120

One hundred times less than £1200

2 marks

Learning Objective:

"I can multiply and divide numbers by 10 or 100 and describe what happens to the digits."

Mental Maths

1 Write in the missing number.

$\boxed{} - 46 = 14$

1 mark

2 A pencil costs 17p. A ruler costs 45p.

What is the total cost of a pencil and a ruler?

$\boxed{ \text{p}}$

1 mark

3 Latika has 62 badges. She gives 25 to her sister.

How many badges does Latika have left?

$\boxed{ \text{badges}}$

1 mark

4 What is the difference between seventy-nine and thirty-eight?

$\boxed{}$

1 mark

5 Katie thinks of a number. She subtracts thirty-two and then subtracts five.

Her answer is eleven. What was her original number?

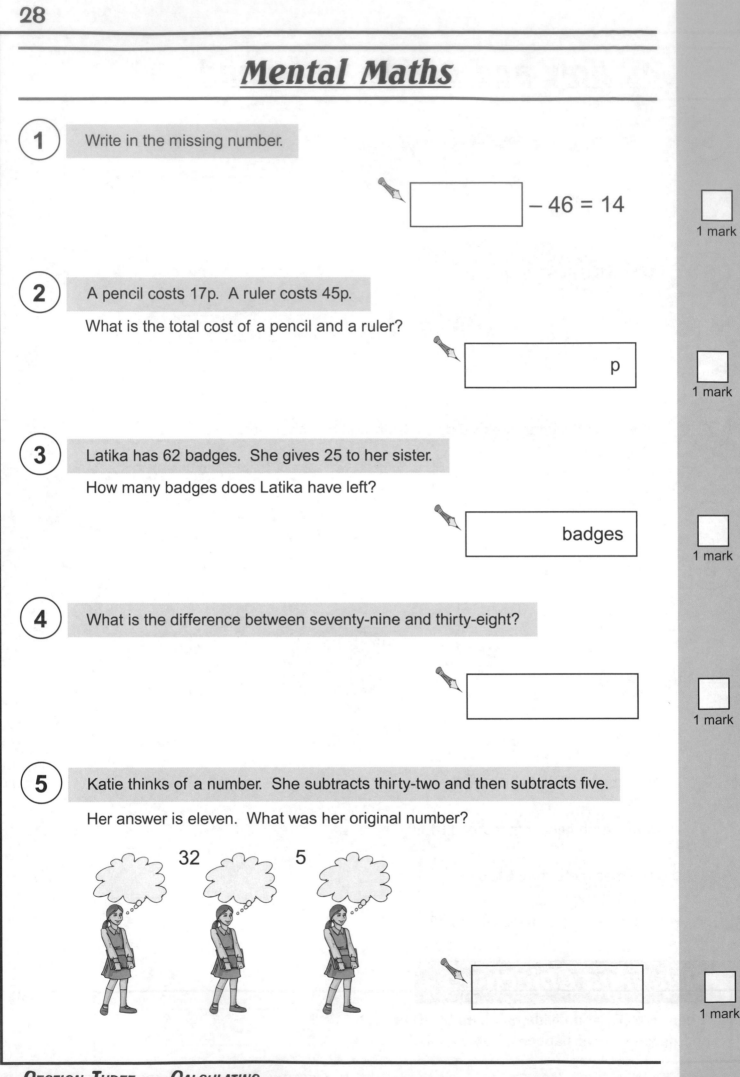

32   5

$\boxed{}$

1 mark

SECTION THREE — CALCULATING

Mental Maths

6 What is the sum of fifty-seven and sixty-four?

1 mark

7 Lee is 57 years old. Anna is 43 years younger than Lee.

How old is Anna?

1 mark

8 Here are the prices for different pieces of fruit.

Banana 49p   Apple 27p   Bunch of Cherries 63p

Write the total cost of the following:

an apple and a bunch of cherries

1 mark

a banana and a bunch of cherries

1 mark

a banana and two apples

1 mark

9 Write in the missing number.

$56 + \boxed{} = 123$

1 mark

Learning Objective:

"I can use mental addition and subtraction to help me solve problems."

Written Adding and Subtracting 1

1 What is two hundred and twenty-four minus fifty-eight?

1 mark

2 Ellen has £36. She is given £47. How much does she have now?

£

1 mark

3 Write in the missing digits.

585 + 3 ☐ 7 = 952   4 ☐ 9 + 316 = 755

2 marks

4 Sophie is 128 cm tall.

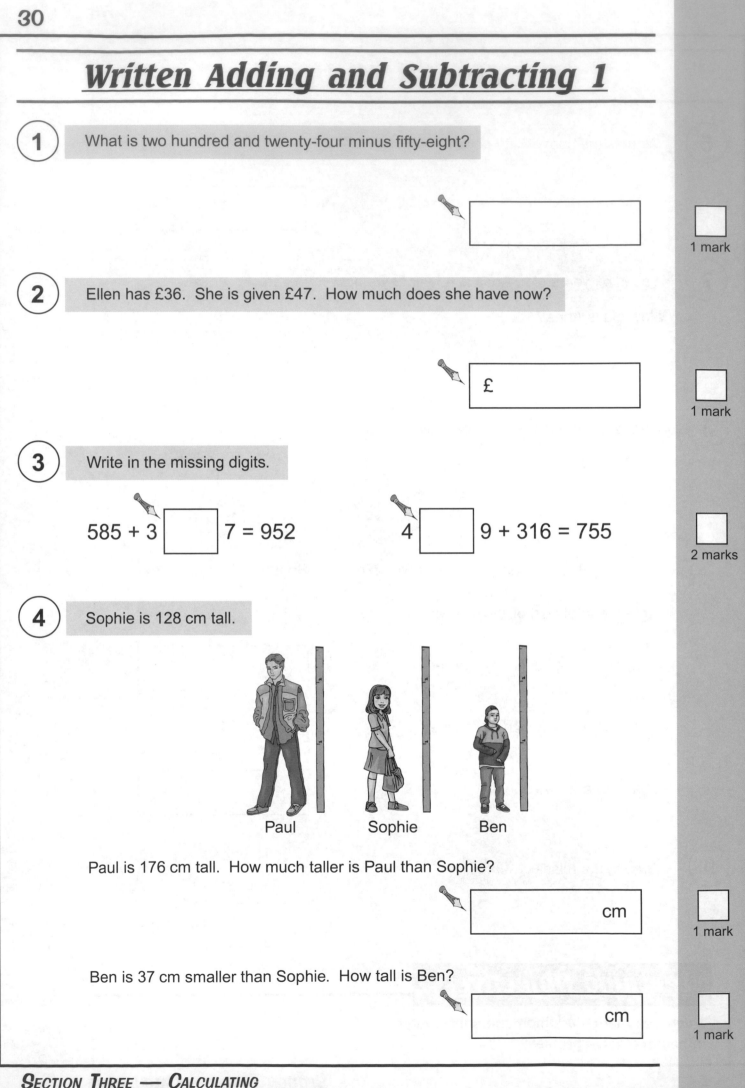

Paul   Sophie   Ben

Paul is 176 cm tall. How much taller is Paul than Sophie?

cm

1 mark

Ben is 37 cm smaller than Sophie. How tall is Ben?

cm

1 mark

Written Adding and Subtracting 1

5 Subtract two hundred and twelve from nine hundred and nine.

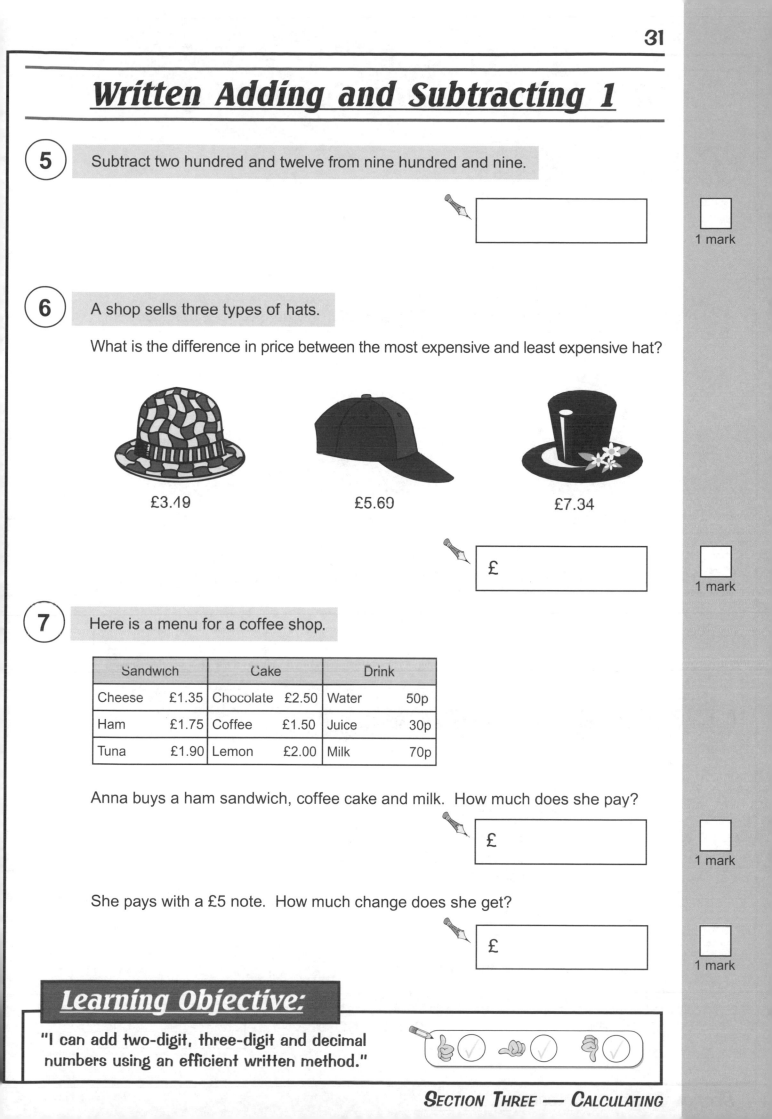

1 mark

6 A shop sells three types of hats.

What is the difference in price between the most expensive and least expensive hat?

£3.19   £5.69   £7.34

£

1 mark

7 Here is a menu for a coffee shop.

Sandwich		Cake		Drink	
Cheese	£1.35	Chocolate	£2.50	Water	50p
Ham	£1.75	Coffee	£1.50	Juice	30p
Tuna	£1.90	Lemon	£2.00	Milk	70p

Anna buys a ham sandwich, coffee cake and milk. How much does she pay?

£

1 mark

She pays with a £5 note. How much change does she get?

£

1 mark

Learning Objective:

"I can add two-digit, three-digit and decimal numbers using an efficient written method."

Written Adding and Subtracting 2

1 Calculate 1342 + 427 + 34.

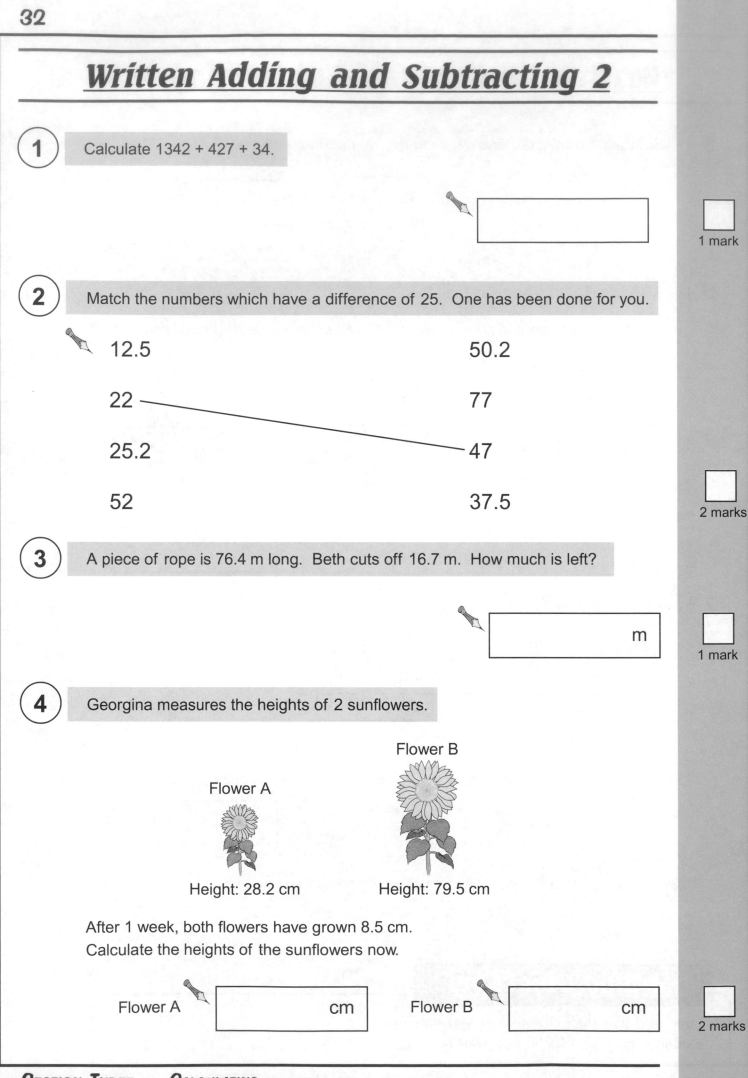

1 mark

2 Match the numbers which have a difference of 25. One has been done for you.

12.5	50.2
22	77
25.2	47
52	37.5

2 marks

3 A piece of rope is 76.4 m long. Beth cuts off 16.7 m. How much is left?

m

1 mark

4 Georgina measures the heights of 2 sunflowers.

Flower B

Flower A

Height: 28.2 cm   Height: 79.5 cm

After 1 week, both flowers have grown 8.5 cm.
Calculate the heights of the sunflowers now.

Flower A   cm   Flower B   cm

2 marks

Written Adding and Subtracting 2

5 Write in the missing digit.

54.2 – 37. ☐ = 16.4

☐ 1 mark

6 Add five point three nine and eight point four six.

☐ 1 mark

7 Calculate the following:

4.36 + 7.69 =

☐ 1 mark

17.25 – 6.43 =

☐ 1 mark

8 Circle the two numbers that add together to make 16.45.

| 9.24 | 8.52 | 9.76 |

| 7.94 | 7.21 | 6.79 |

☐ 1 mark

Learning Objective:

"I can add two-digit, three-digit and decimal numbers using an efficient written method."

Written Multiplying and Dividing

1 Work out 35 × 41.

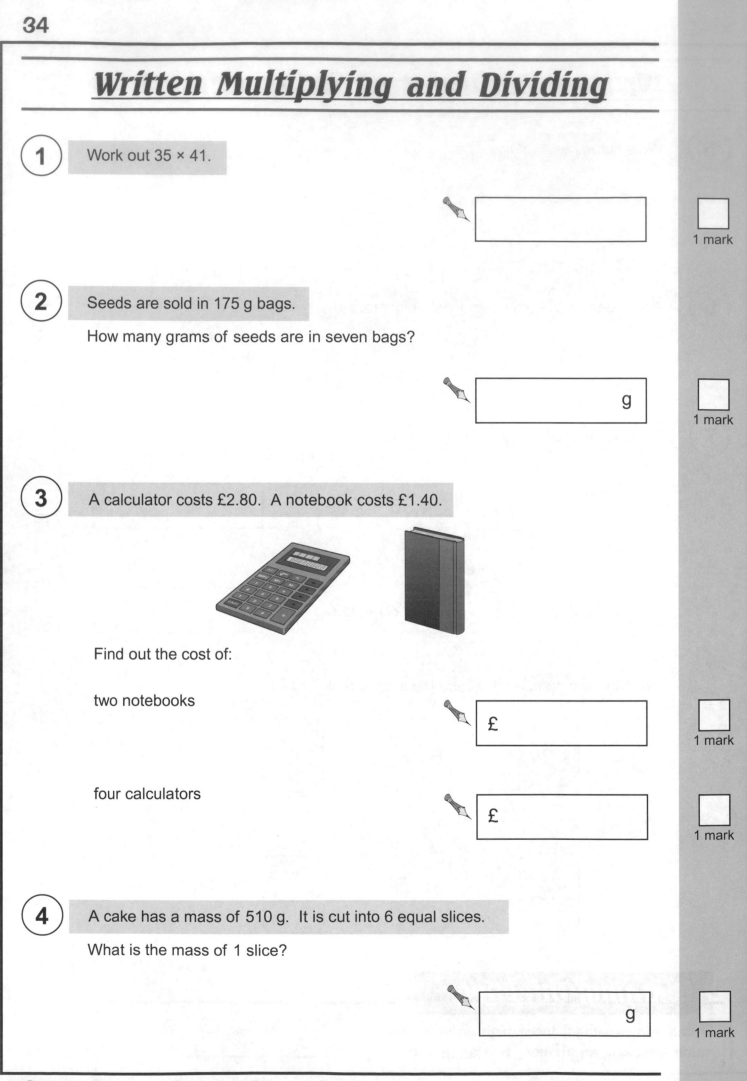

1 mark

2 Seeds are sold in 175 g bags.

How many grams of seeds are in seven bags?

g

1 mark

3 A calculator costs £2.80. A notebook costs £1.40.

Find out the cost of:

two notebooks

£

1 mark

four calculators

£

1 mark

4 A cake has a mass of 510 g. It is cut into 6 equal slices.

What is the mass of 1 slice?

g

1 mark

Written Multiplying and Dividing

(5) Calculate 392 ÷ 7.

1 mark

(6) Work out 9.7 × 3.

1 mark

(7) David's dog eats one tin of food a day. Each tin costs 47p.

How much would it cost to feed the dog for:

twelve days?

£

1 mark

nineteen days?

£

1 mark

(8) Write in the missing digits to complete this multiplication.

```
    □ 4 □
  ×     5
  ─────────
  1 2 3 0
```

1 mark

Learning Objective:

"I can solve multiplication and division calculations using written methods."

Calculators

1   Fiona saves £2.40 a week for 18 weeks. How much money does she save?

£ ☐

☐ 1 mark

2   Write in the missing digits.

$$
\begin{array}{r}
2 \quad 9 \quad \boxed{} \\
+ \quad 1 \quad \boxed{} \quad 9 \\
\hline
4 \quad 8 \quad 6
\end{array}
$$

☐ 1 mark

3   What is the difference between 25.7 and 31.9?

☐

☐ 1 mark

4   A bottle of medicine holds 675 ml. One dose is 5 ml.

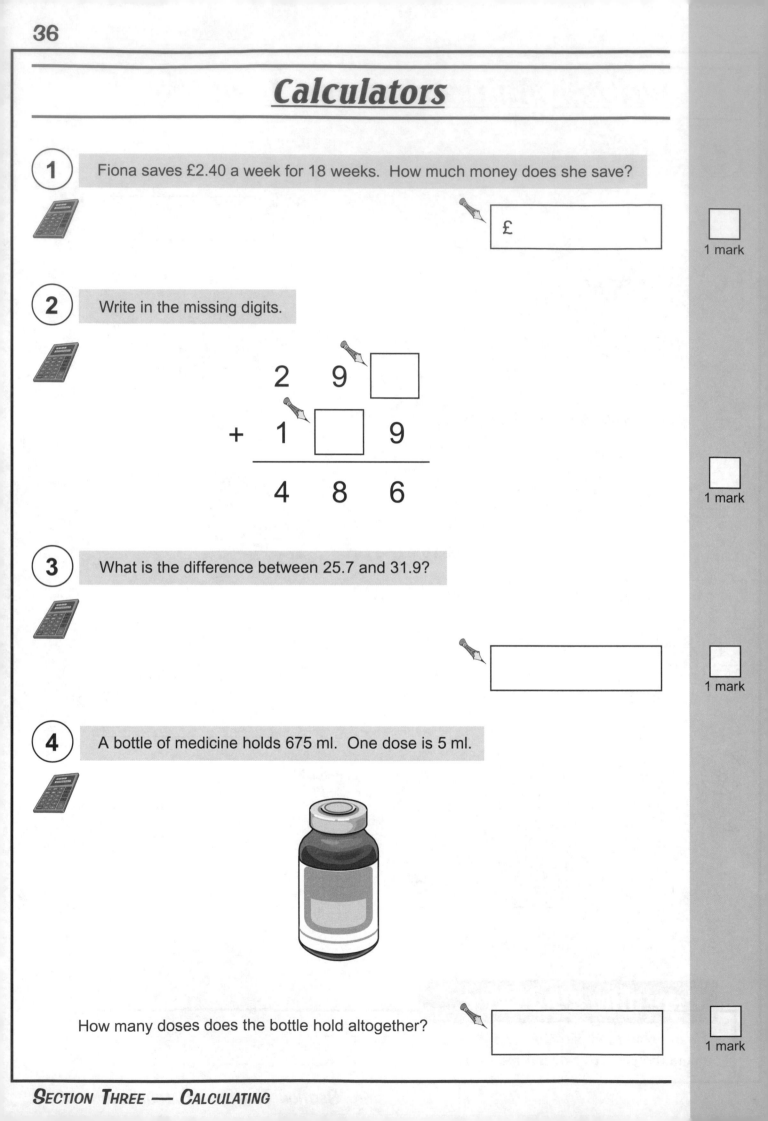

How many doses does the bottle hold altogether? ☐

☐ 1 mark

Calculators

5   A box contains 80 pencils. The box and pencils have a total mass of 365 g.

The empty box has a mass of 45 g. Find the mass of one pencil.

g

6   John is 178 cm tall. Dan is 94 cm tall.

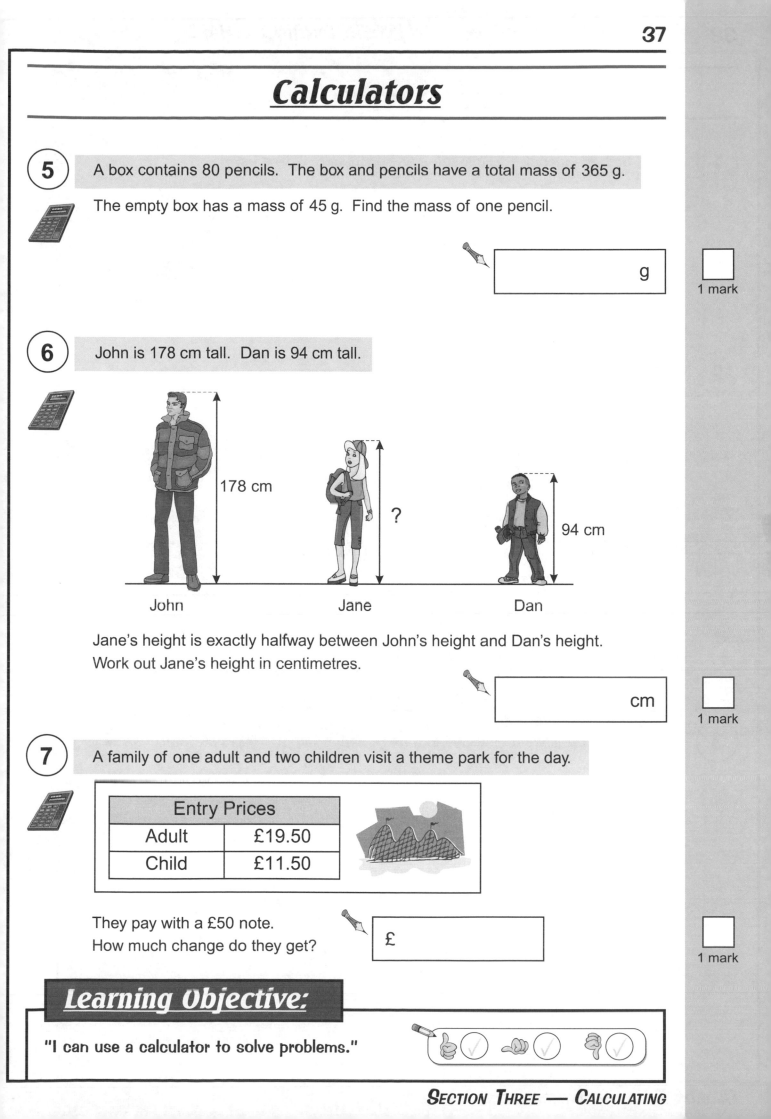

178 cm

?

94 cm

John   Jane   Dan

Jane's height is exactly halfway between John's height and Dan's height.
Work out Jane's height in centimetres.

cm

7   A family of one adult and two children visit a theme park for the day.

Entry Prices	
Adult	£19.50
Child	£11.50

They pay with a £50 note.
How much change do they get?

£

Learning Objective:

"I can use a calculator to solve problems."

2D Shapes

1 Look at these triangles. Circle the triangles that are isosceles.

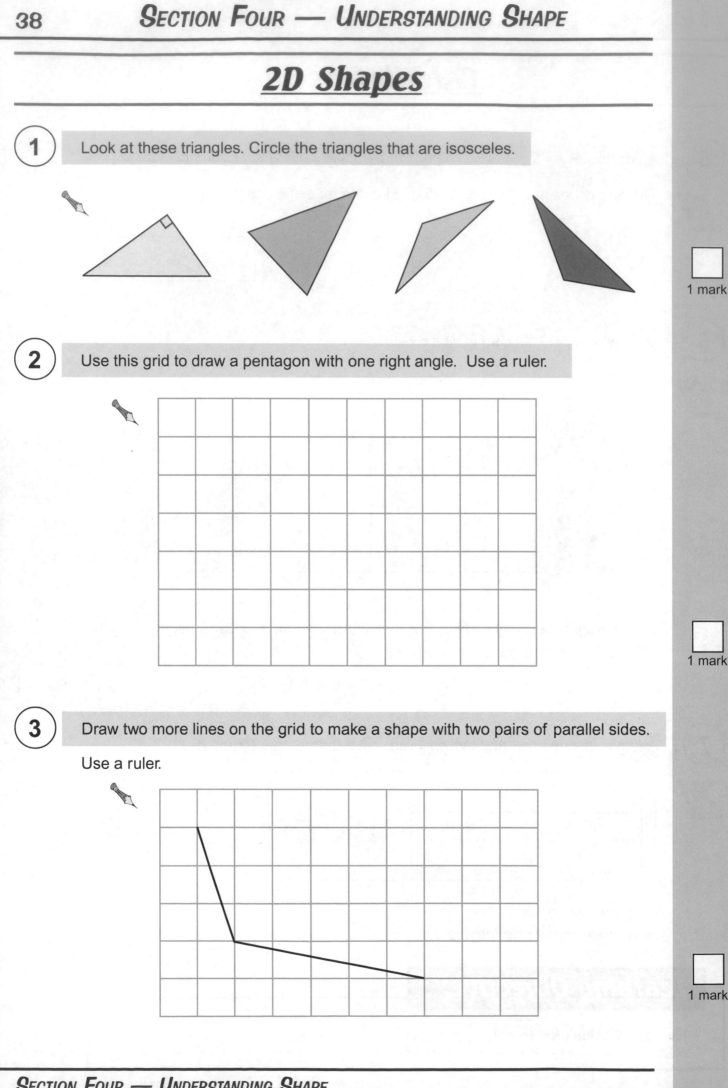

1 mark

2 Use this grid to draw a pentagon with one right angle. Use a ruler.

1 mark

3 Draw two more lines on the grid to make a shape with two pairs of parallel sides.

Use a ruler.

1 mark

2D Shapes

4 Here is a regular pentagon.

Join three dots to make an isosceles triangle.
Use a ruler.

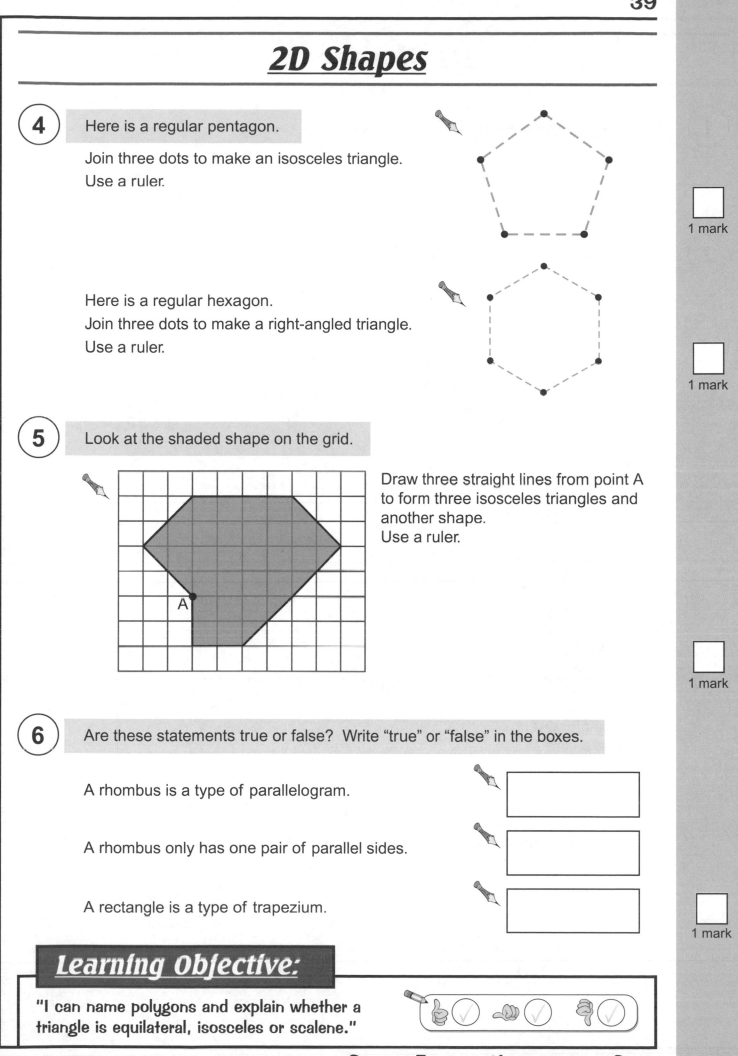

1 mark

Here is a regular hexagon.
Join three dots to make a right-angled triangle.
Use a ruler.

1 mark

5 Look at the shaded shape on the grid.

Draw three straight lines from point A to form three isosceles triangles and another shape.
Use a ruler.

A

1 mark

6 Are these statements true or false? Write "true" or "false" in the boxes.

A rhombus is a type of parallelogram.

A rhombus only has one pair of parallel sides.

A rectangle is a type of trapezium.

1 mark

Learning Objective:

"I can name polygons and explain whether a triangle is equilateral, isosceles or scalene."

3D Shapes

1 How many edges does a tetrahedron have?

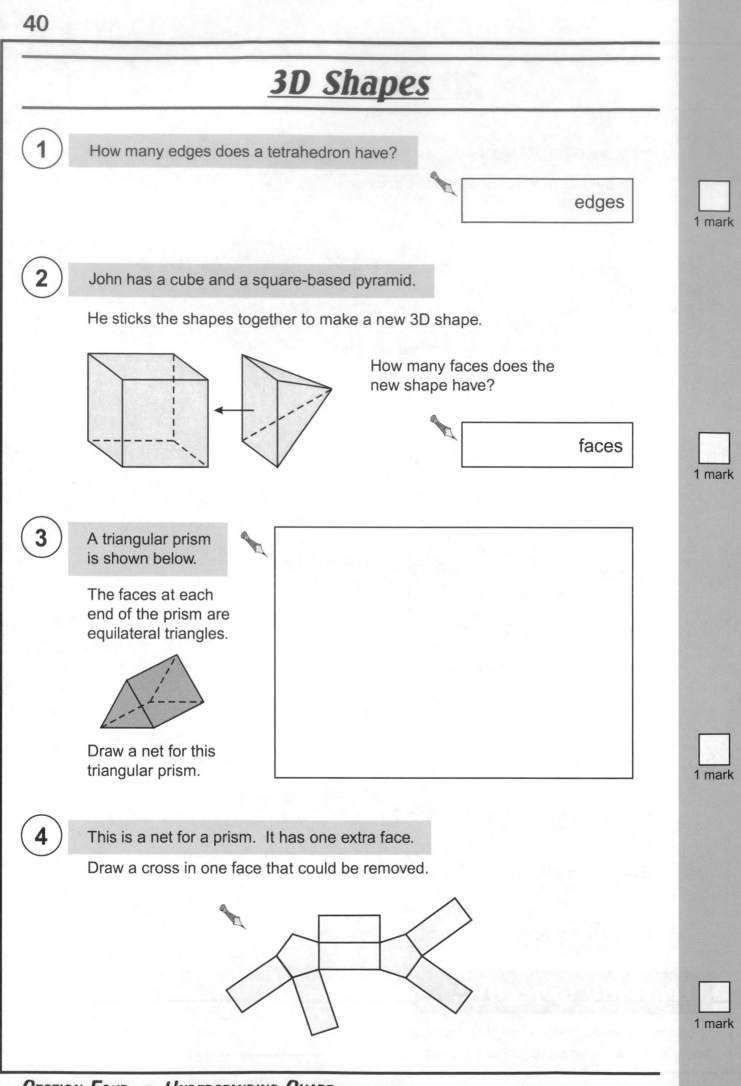

_____ edges

1 mark

2 John has a cube and a square-based pyramid.

He sticks the shapes together to make a new 3D shape.

How many faces does the new shape have?

_____ faces

1 mark

3 A triangular prism is shown below.

The faces at each end of the prism are equilateral triangles.

Draw a net for this triangular prism.

1 mark

4 This is a net for a prism. It has one extra face.

Draw a cross in one face that could be removed.

1 mark

3D Shapes

5 A prism with end face A has been drawn on the grid.

Use the grid to draw prisms that have end faces B and C.

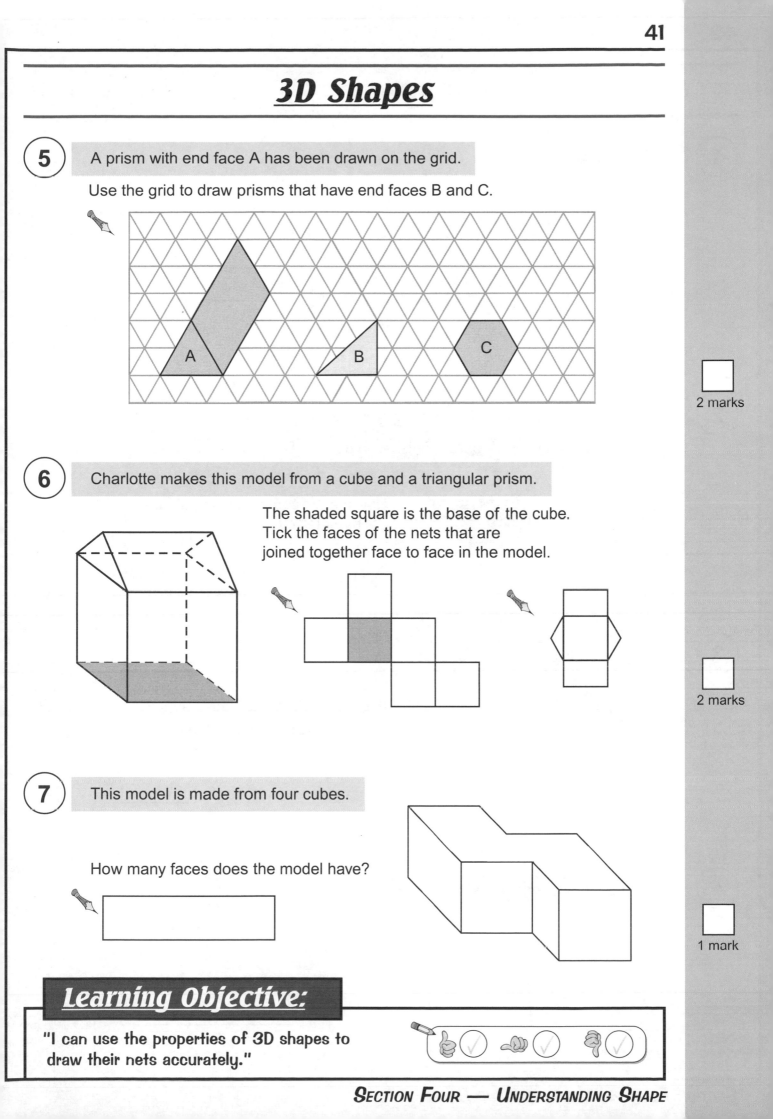

2 marks

6 Charlotte makes this model from a cube and a triangular prism.

The shaded square is the base of the cube.
Tick the faces of the nets that are
joined together face to face in the model.

2 marks

7 This model is made from four cubes.

How many faces does the model have?

1 mark

SECTION FOUR — UNDERSTANDING SHAPE

Angles

1 Use a protractor to measure these angles accurately.

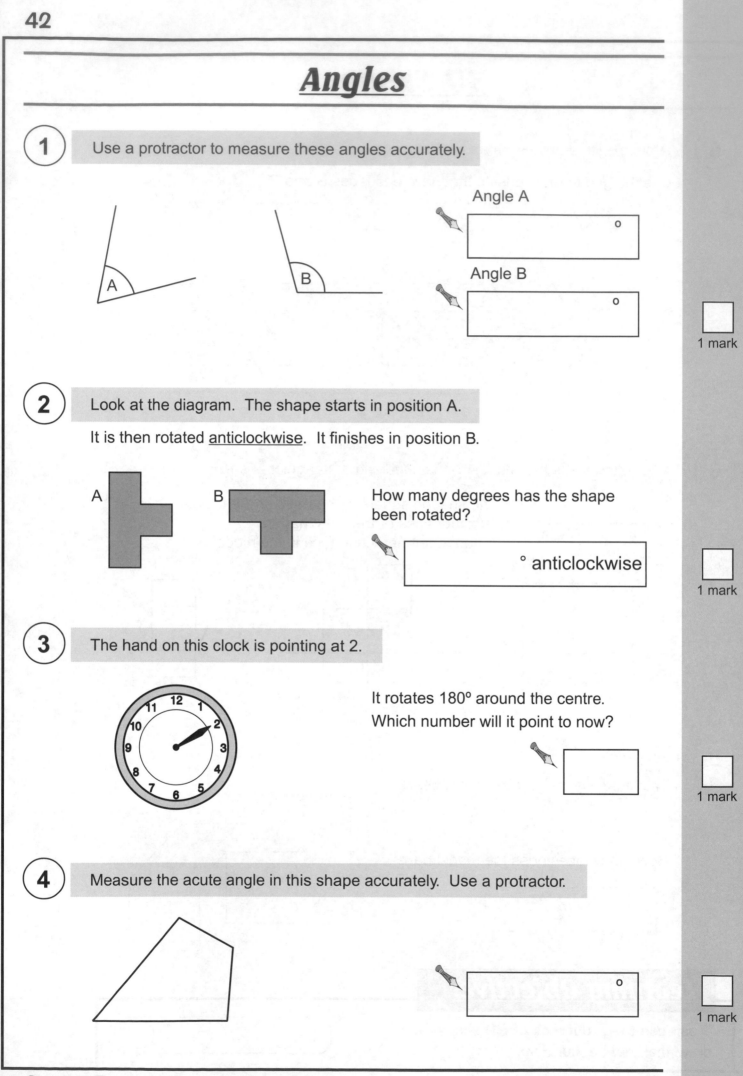

Angle A

⬛ °

Angle B

⬛ °

1 mark

2 Look at the diagram. The shape starts in position A.

It is then rotated <u>anticlockwise</u>. It finishes in position B.

A

B

How many degrees has the shape been rotated?

⬛ ° anticlockwise

1 mark

3 The hand on this clock is pointing at 2.

It rotates 180° around the centre. Which number will it point to now?

⬛

1 mark

4 Measure the acute angle in this shape accurately. Use a protractor.

⬛ °

1 mark

Angles

5 Write the letters of the angles in order of size. Start with the smallest.

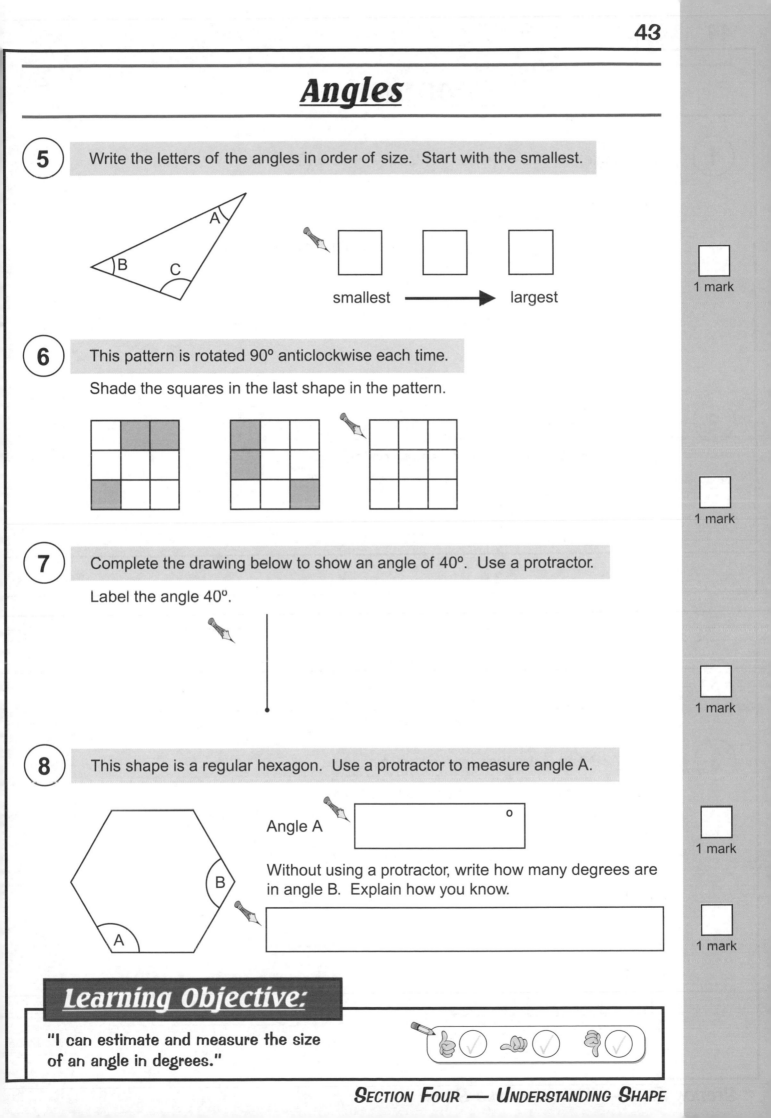

smallest ──────▶ largest

1 mark

6 This pattern is rotated 90° anticlockwise each time.

Shade the squares in the last shape in the pattern.

1 mark

7 Complete the drawing below to show an angle of 40°. Use a protractor.

Label the angle 40°.

1 mark

8 This shape is a regular hexagon. Use a protractor to measure angle A.

Angle A [°   ]

1 mark

Without using a protractor, write how many degrees are in angle B. Explain how you know.

1 mark

Learning Objective:

"I can estimate and measure the size of an angle in degrees."

Coordinates

1 A rectangle has three vertices at (2, 4), (2, 6) and (5,4).

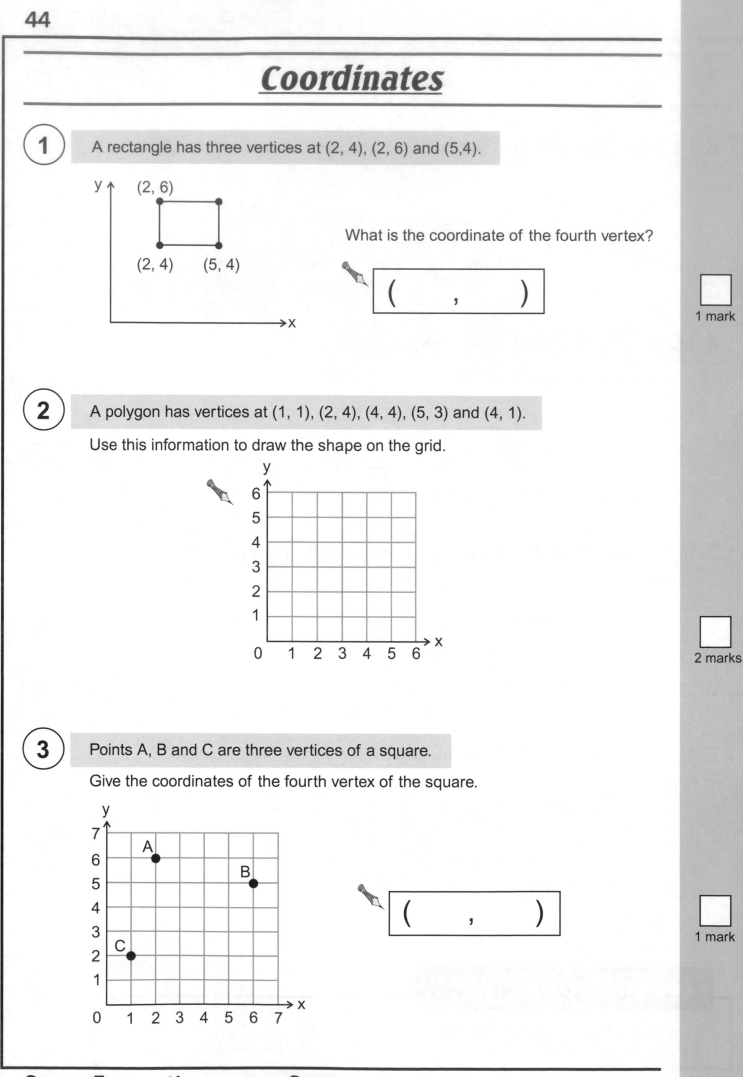

What is the coordinate of the fourth vertex?

(,   )

1 mark

2 A polygon has vertices at (1, 1), (2, 4), (4, 4), (5, 3) and (4, 1).

Use this information to draw the shape on the grid.

2 marks

3 Points A, B and C are three vertices of a square.

Give the coordinates of the fourth vertex of the square.

(,   )

1 mark

Coordinates

4 Look at this map.

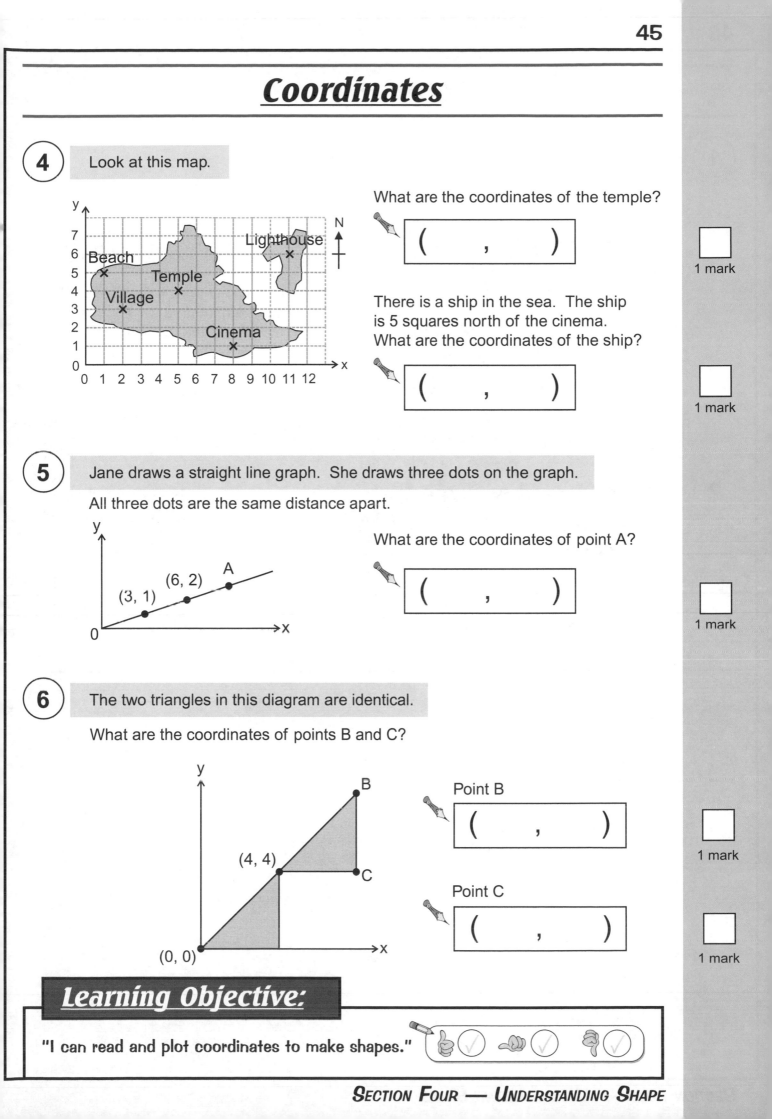

What are the coordinates of the temple?

(,)

1 mark

There is a ship in the sea. The ship is 5 squares north of the cinema. What are the coordinates of the ship?

(,)

1 mark

5 Jane draws a straight line graph. She draws three dots on the graph.

All three dots are the same distance apart.

What are the coordinates of point A?

(,)

1 mark

6 The two triangles in this diagram are identical.

What are the coordinates of points B and C?

Point B

(,)

1 mark

Point C

(,)

1 mark

Learning Objective:

"I can read and plot coordinates to make shapes."

Symmetry

1 Look at these shapes.

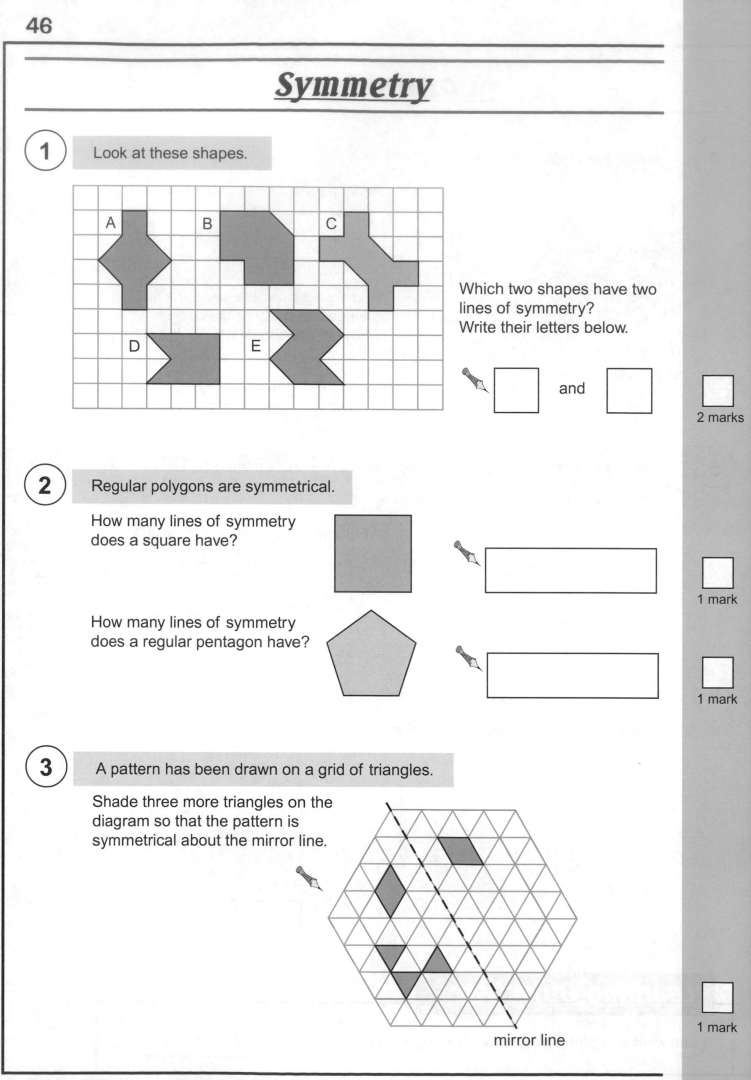

Which two shapes have two lines of symmetry?
Write their letters below.

[ ] and [ ]

[ ] 2 marks

2 Regular polygons are symmetrical.

How many lines of symmetry does a square have?

[   ]

[ ] 1 mark

How many lines of symmetry does a regular pentagon have?

[   ]

[ ] 1 mark

3 A pattern has been drawn on a grid of triangles.

Shade three more triangles on the diagram so that the pattern is symmetrical about the mirror line.

mirror line

[ ] 1 mark

Symmetry

4 The dots on the grid are four vertices of a hexagon.

The hexagon is symmetrical about the dashed mirror line.
Complete the hexagon. Two sides have been drawn for you. Use a ruler.

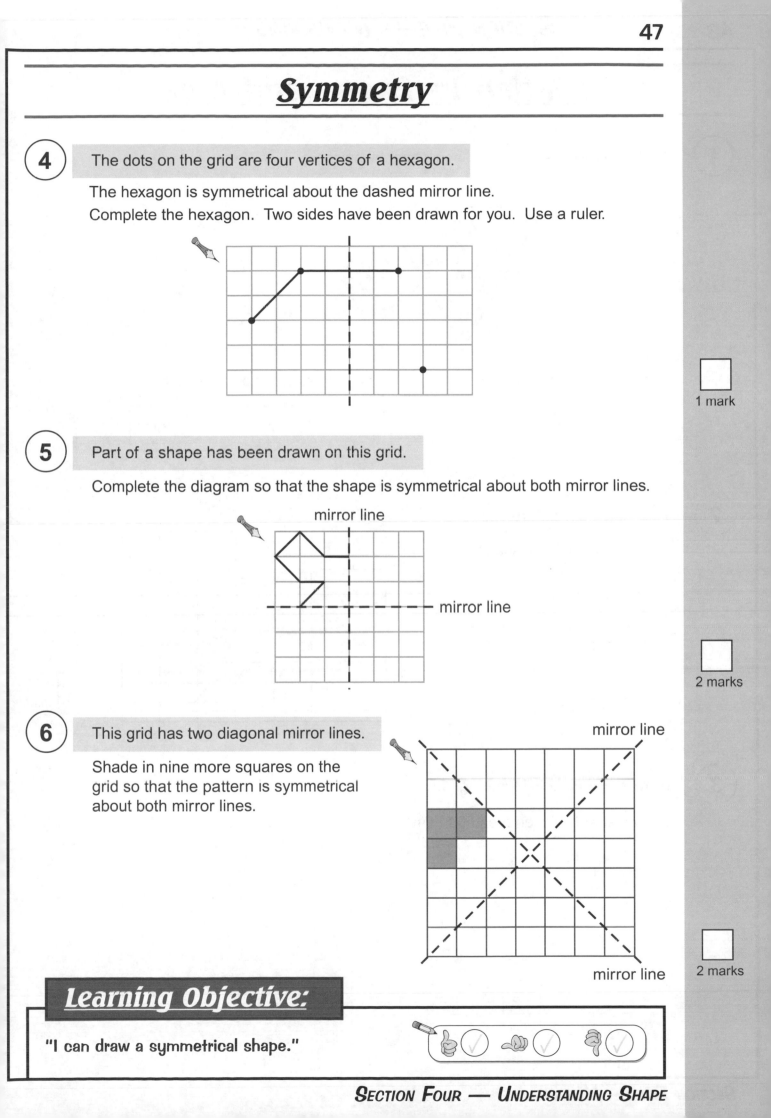

1 mark

5 Part of a shape has been drawn on this grid.

Complete the diagram so that the shape is symmetrical about both mirror lines.

mirror line

mirror line

2 marks

6 This grid has two diagonal mirror lines.

Shade in nine more squares on the grid so that the pattern is symmetrical about both mirror lines.

mirror line

mirror line

2 marks

Learning Objective:

"I can draw a symmetrical shape."

Calculating Perimeter and Area

1 Leona makes a shape using equilateral triangles.

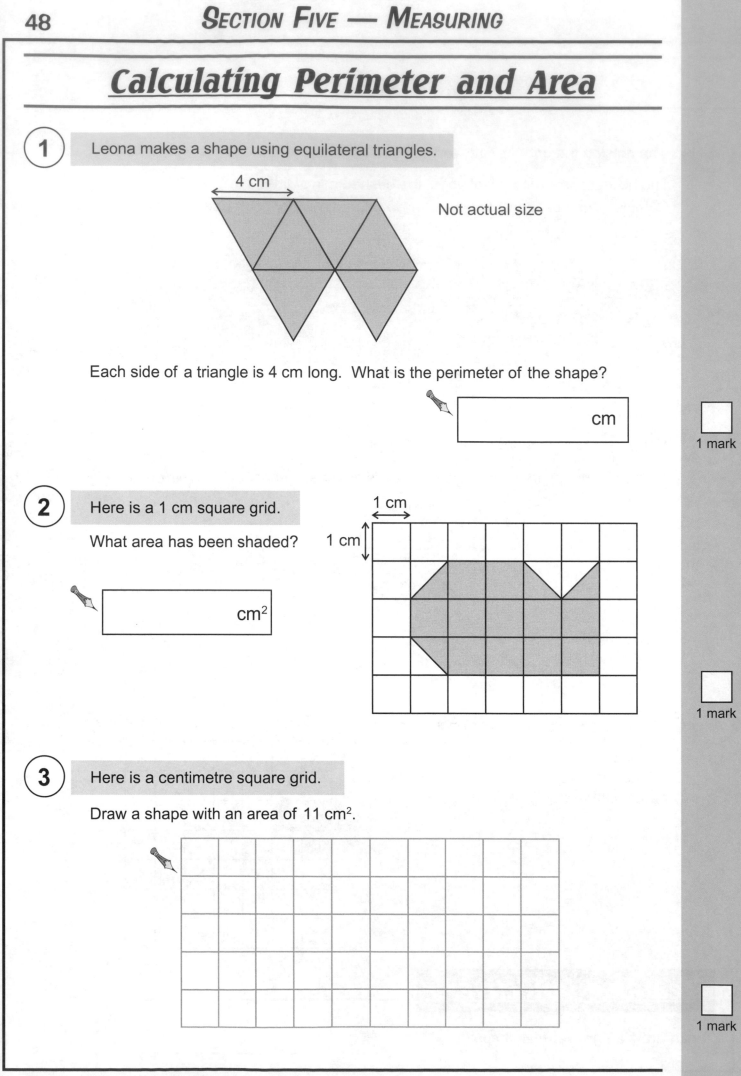

4 cm

Not actual size

Each side of a triangle is 4 cm long. What is the perimeter of the shape?

cm

1 mark

2 Here is a 1 cm square grid.

What area has been shaded?

cm²

1 cm

1 cm

1 mark

3 Here is a centimetre square grid.

Draw a shape with an area of 11 cm².

1 mark

Calculating Perimeter and Area

4 A rectangle has a length of 8 m and a perimeter of 22 m.

Find the width of the rectangle. Show your working.

m

2 marks

5 These five shapes have been drawn on a grid.

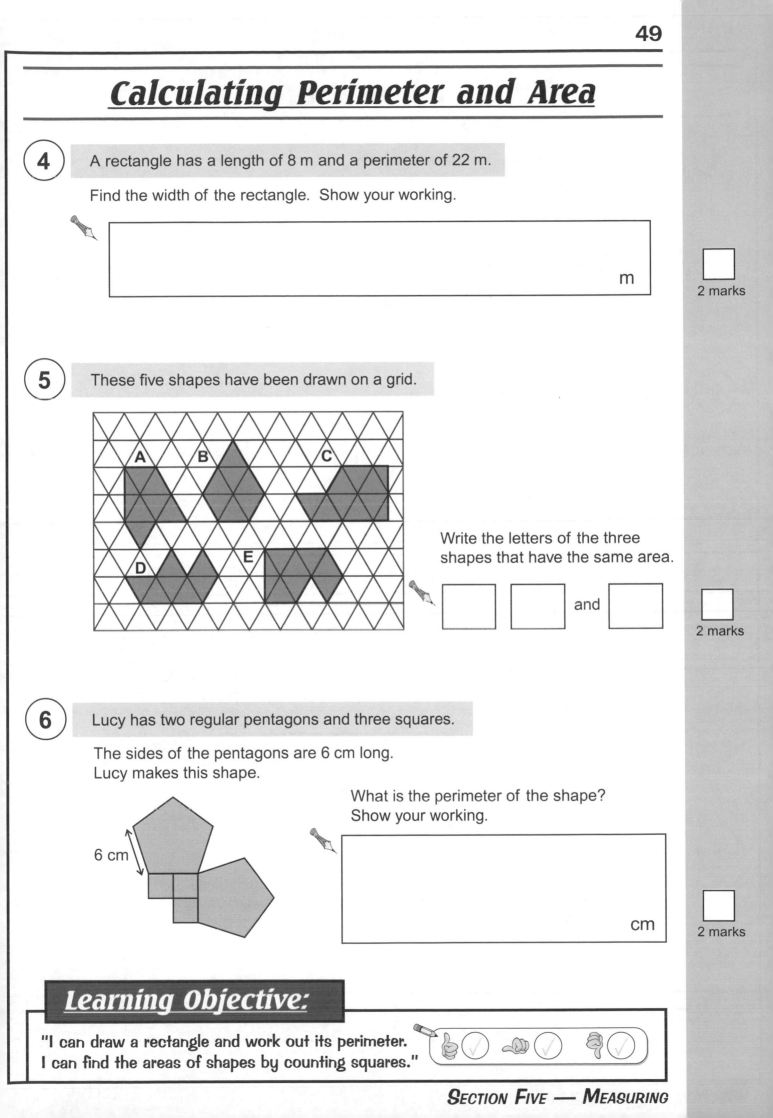

Write the letters of the three shapes that have the same area.

[ ] [ ] and [ ]

2 marks

6 Lucy has two regular pentagons and three squares.

The sides of the pentagons are 6 cm long.
Lucy makes this shape.

6 cm

What is the perimeter of the shape?
Show your working.

cm

2 marks

Learning Objective:

"I can draw a rectangle and work out its perimeter.
I can find the areas of shapes by counting squares."

Units and Measures

1 Circle the correct amount for each sentence.

The length of a car is about:

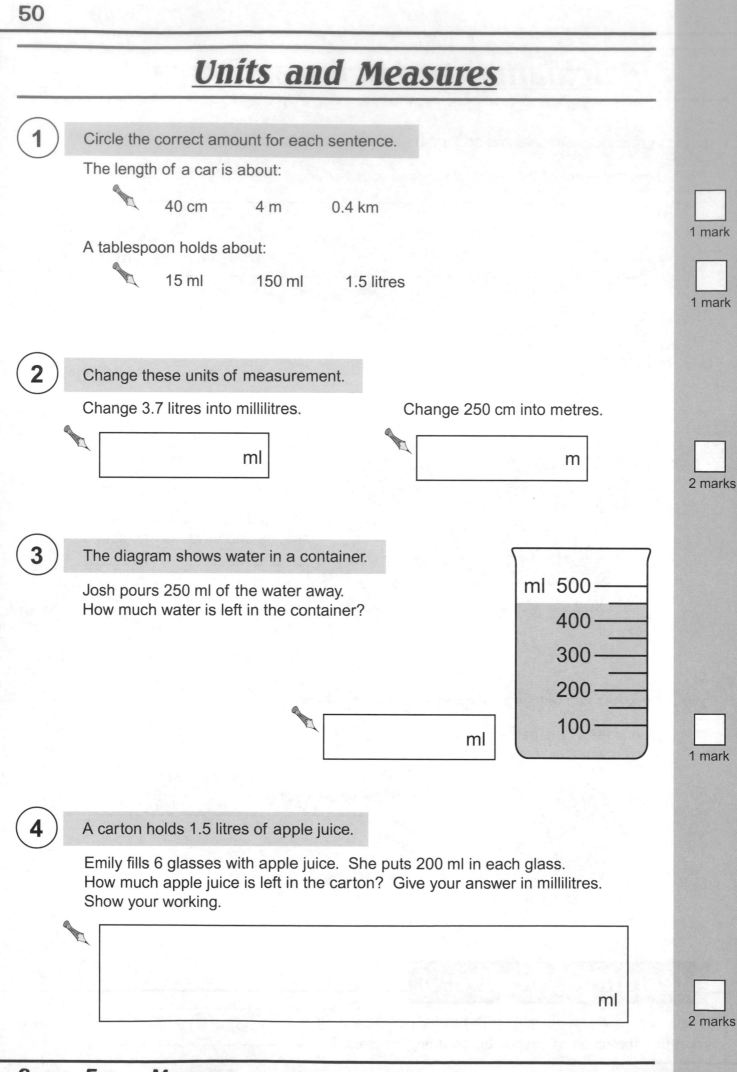 40 cm   4 m   0.4 km

☐ 1 mark

A tablespoon holds about:

15 ml   150 ml   1.5 litres

☐ 1 mark

2 Change these units of measurement.

Change 3.7 litres into millilitres.

☐ ml

Change 250 cm into metres.

☐ m

☐ 2 marks

3 The diagram shows water in a container.

Josh pours 250 ml of the water away.
How much water is left in the container?

☐ ml

ml 500
400
300
200
100

☐ 1 mark

4 A carton holds 1.5 litres of apple juice.

Emily fills 6 glasses with apple juice. She puts 200 ml in each glass.
How much apple juice is left in the carton? Give your answer in millilitres.
Show your working.

☐ ml

☐ 2 marks

Units and Measures

5 Sayeed uses a centimetre ruler to measure two paper clips and a coin.

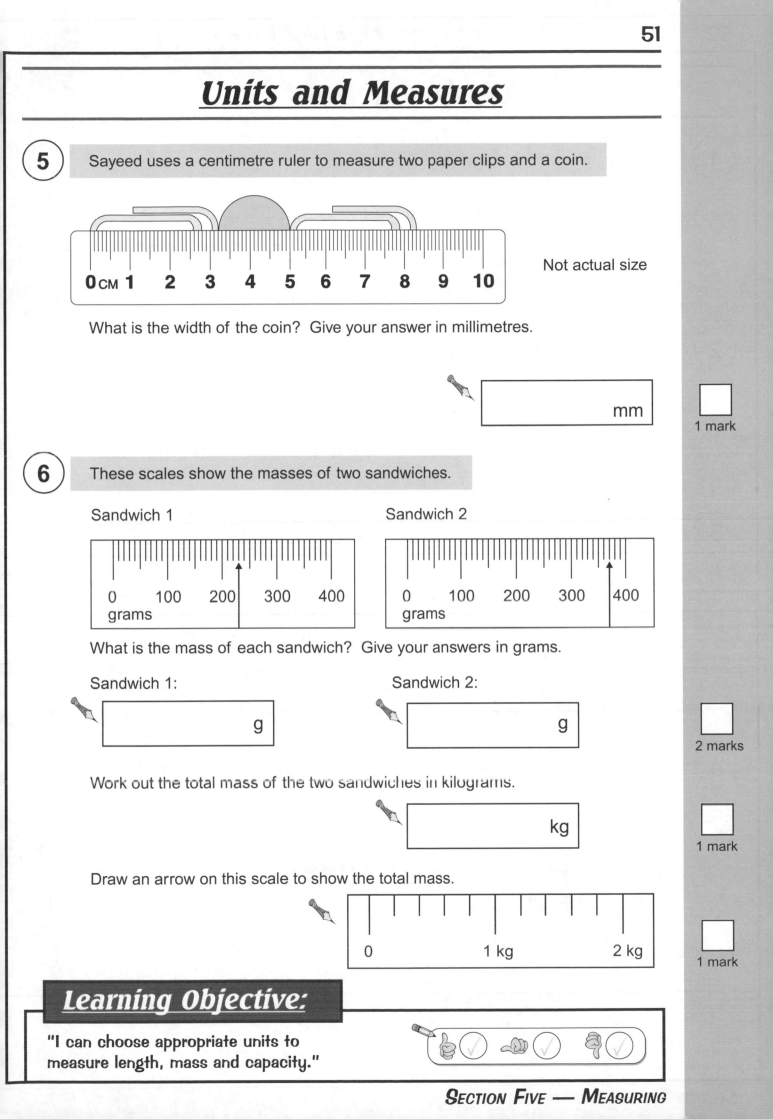

Not actual size

What is the width of the coin? Give your answer in millimetres.

mm

1 mark

6 These scales show the masses of two sandwiches.

Sandwich 1

0   100   200   300   400
grams

Sandwich 2

0   100   200   300   400
grams

What is the mass of each sandwich? Give your answers in grams.

Sandwich 1:

g

Sandwich 2:

g

2 marks

Work out the total mass of the two sandwiches in kilograms.

kg

1 mark

Draw an arrow on this scale to show the total mass.

0   1 kg   2 kg

1 mark

Learning Objective:

"I can choose appropriate units to measure length, mass and capacity."

SECTION FIVE — MEASURING

Analysing Data

1 Find the mode of each set of data:

5 2 3 2 1 2 3 4 4

Red, Blue, Blue, Green, Yellow

1 mark

1 mark

2 I rolled a dice six times. The mode was 4.

Circle all the possible sets of values for the six throws.

4 2 2 4 4 1　　　1 2 4 5 4 4　　　6 3 2 5 4 4

1 4 3 2 5 5　　　4 4 4 4 6 6　　　5 2 5 5 6 3

2 marks

3 Kiera recorded how she went to school every day for a month.

Method	Frequency
Bus	6
Car	5
Walking	9

Which way of getting to school was the mode?

1 mark

4 Serge has made a bar chart showing the colours of his classmates' eyes.

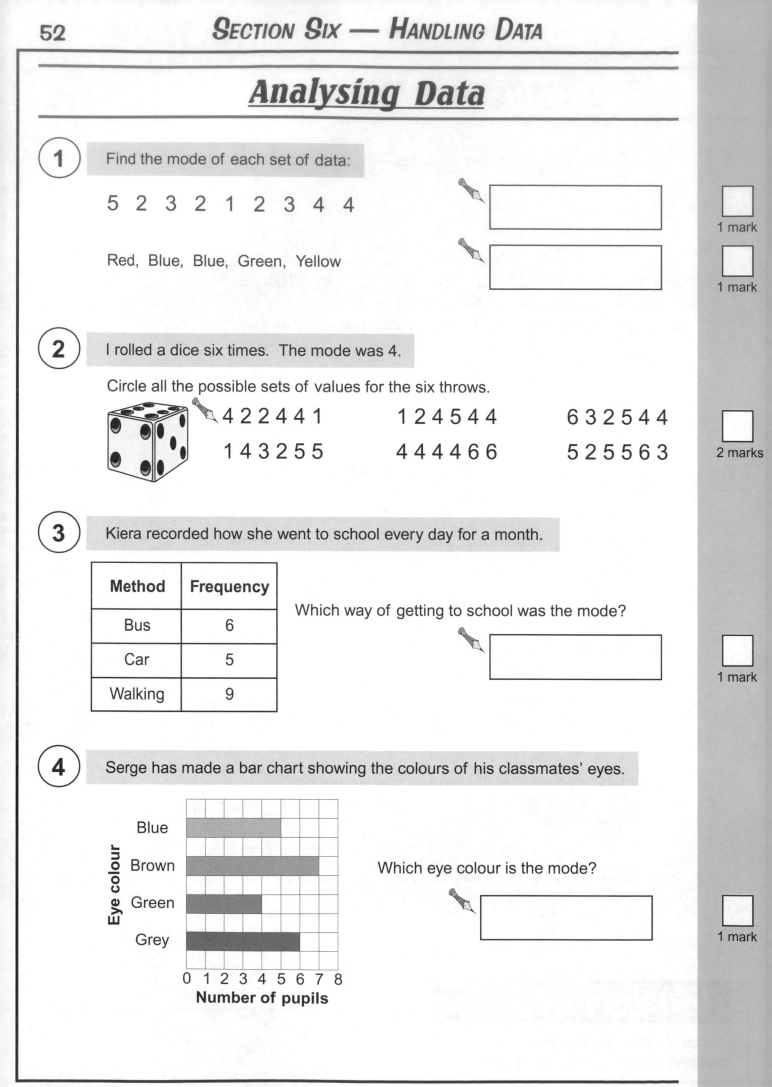

Which eye colour is the mode?

1 mark

Analysing Data

5 Karen rolls a dice 100 times. She writes down the score every time.

Circle the most likely range of her data.

99   5   17   4   24

1 mark

6 Look at this set of data.   9 9 4 11 2 7 5 12

What is the mode?

1 mark

What is the range?

1 mark

7 Tyler recorded the number of hours he spent watching TV each day.

The lowest number of hours he watched was half an hour.
The range of his data was three and a half hours.

What was the greatest number of hours he watched TV in a day?
Show your working.

hours

2 marks

8 Harriet asked her class how many films they had watched over the weekend.

She found that 4 classmates had watched no films,
10 had watched one film, and 8 had watched two films.

What was the mode number of films watched?

1 mark

Learning Objective:

"I can find the mode and the range of a set of data."

Chance and Likelihood

1   Bobby has a bag of marbles.

In the bag he has 10 blue marbles, 8 red marbles and 1 green marble.
He picks out a marble without looking.

Is it CERTAIN, LIKELY, UNLIKELY or IMPOSSIBLE that:

The marble picked is brown?

1 mark

The marble picked is blue or red?

1 mark

2   Calvin says it's going to snow tomorrow.

Is Calvin more likely to be correct if:

It's winter or spring?

1 mark

He lives in Iceland or Spain?

1 mark

3   Maxine likes jazz music. Dennis likes to play golf. Mark doesn't like jazz or golf.

Are you MORE LIKELY or LESS LIKELY to find Mark playing golf than Dennis?

1 mark

Who are you most likely to find listening to a jazz band?

1 mark

Look at the picture on the left.

Who is most likely to own this?

1 mark

Chance and Likelihood

4 I roll a normal six-sided dice. Write how likely each event is.

Choose from: impossible, unlikely, likely or certain.

I get a number less than seven.

I get a number more than six.

5 Nikos has a pet rabbit.

Label each of these events as **most** likely, **least** likely or in the **middle**.

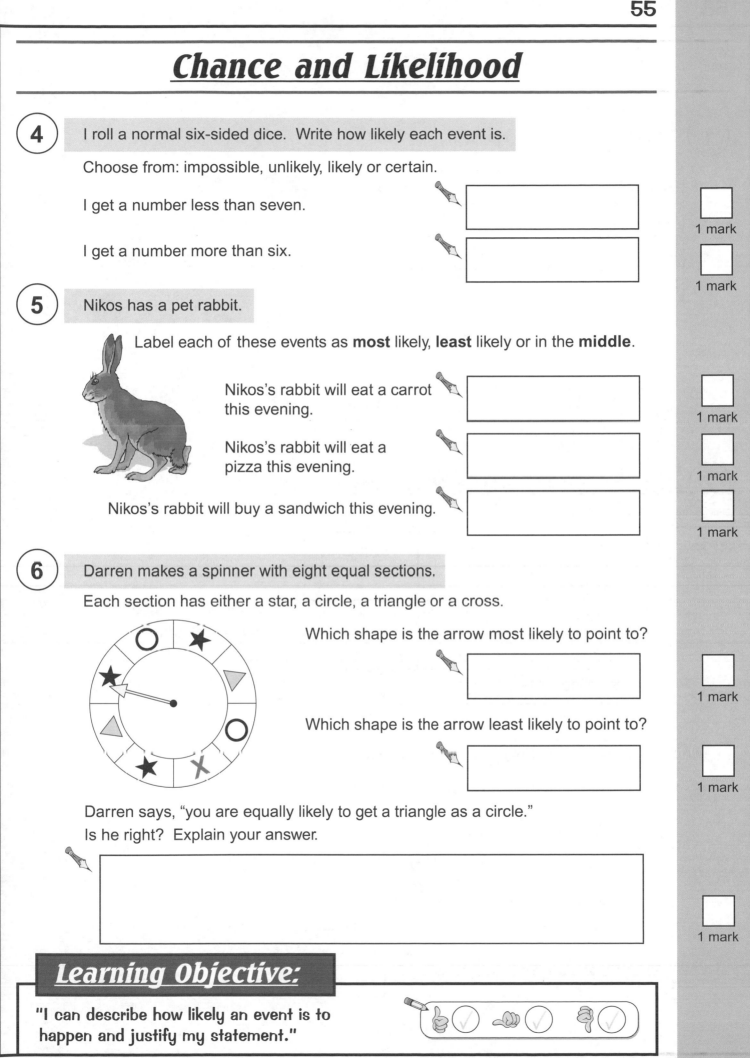

Nikos's rabbit will eat a carrot this evening.

1 mark

Nikos's rabbit will eat a pizza this evening.

1 mark

Nikos's rabbit will buy a sandwich this evening.

1 mark

6 Darren makes a spinner with eight equal sections.

Each section has either a star, a circle, a triangle or a cross.

Which shape is the arrow most likely to point to?

1 mark

Which shape is the arrow least likely to point to?

1 mark

Darren says, "you are equally likely to get a triangle as a circle."
Is he right? Explain your answer.

1 mark

Learning Objective:

"I can describe how likely an event is to happen and justify my statement."

Data

1 Use the picture to complete the tally chart.

Animal	Tally	Frequency
Cat		
Dog		
Rabbit		

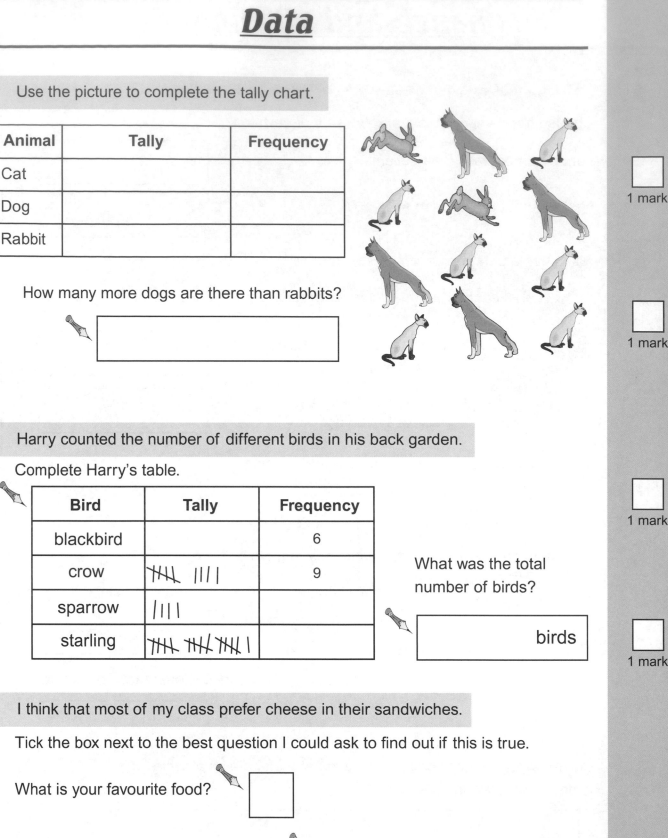

1 mark

How many more dogs are there than rabbits?

1 mark

2 Harry counted the number of different birds in his back garden.

Complete Harry's table.

Bird	Tally	Frequency
blackbird		6
crow	ⅢⅢ ⅢⅠ	9
sparrow	ⅢⅠ	
starling	ⅢⅢ ⅢⅢ ⅢⅢ Ⅰ	

1 mark

What was the total number of birds?

_____ birds

1 mark

3 I think that most of my class prefer cheese in their sandwiches.

Tick the box next to the best question I could ask to find out if this is true.

What is your favourite food? ☐

What is your favourite sandwich filling? ☐

What did you eat for lunch today? ☐

1 mark

Data

4 Rachel records the colours of the cars that pass her school.

Here are her results.

blue	red	blue	green	silver	red	blue	silver	green	green
red	blue	green	red	red	red	blue	silver	green	green	red
green	silver	green	blue	blue	silver	red	red	blue	red

Construct and label a tally chart to present this information.

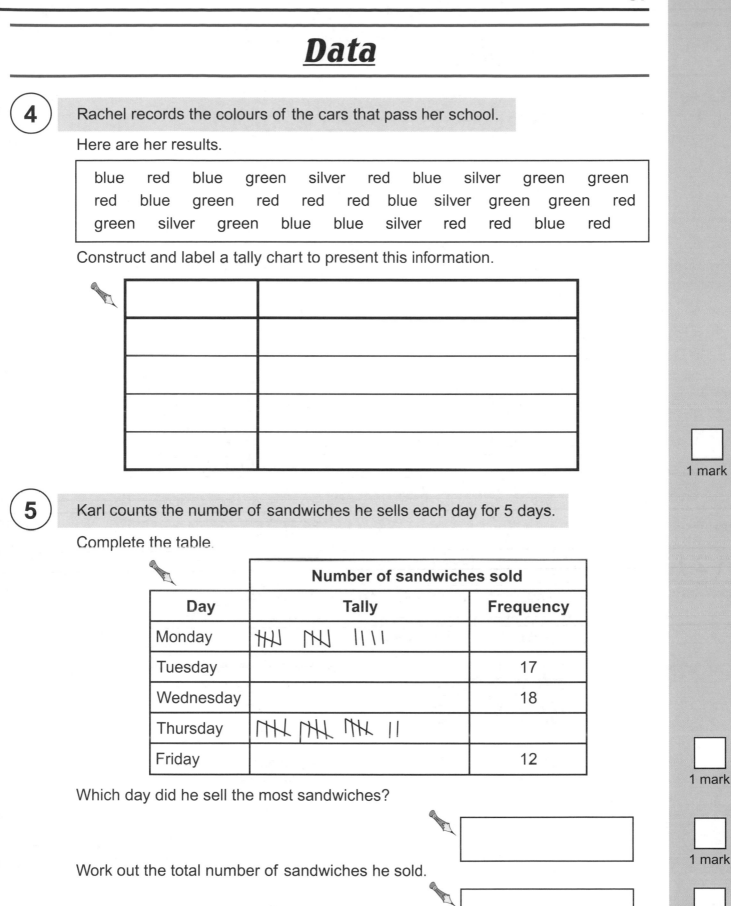

1 mark

5 Karl counts the number of sandwiches he sells each day for 5 days.

Complete the table.

	Number of sandwiches sold	
Day	**Tally**	**Frequency**
Monday	ЦЖ ЦЖ IIII	
Tuesday		17
Wednesday		18
Thursday	ЦЖ ЦЖ ЦЖ II	
Friday		12

1 mark

Which day did he sell the most sandwiches?

1 mark

Work out the total number of sandwiches he sold.

1 mark

SECTION SIX — HANDLING DATA

Tables and Charts 1

1 This table shows the numbers of different fish that Emma sold.

Use this table to complete the bar chart.

Fish	Number sold
Cod	20
Haddock	14
Plaice	9
Skate	16

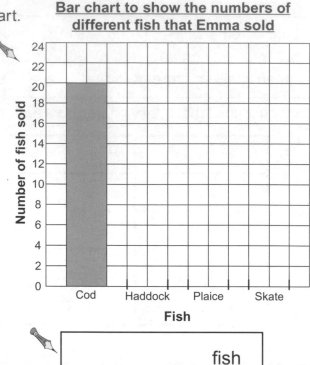

Bar chart to show the numbers of different fish that Emma sold

What was the total number of fish that Emma sold?

[   ] fish

1 mark

1 mark

2 Ed sells four flavours of crisps at his café.

He records the number of each flavour he sold in a bar chart.

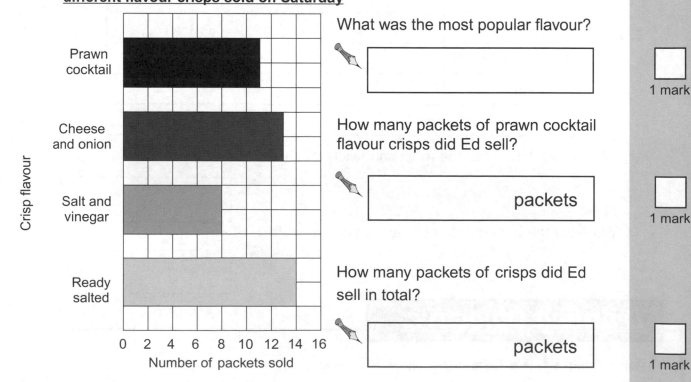

Bar chart to show the numbers of different flavour crisps sold on Saturday

What was the most popular flavour?

[   ]

1 mark

How many packets of prawn cocktail flavour crisps did Ed sell?

[   ] packets

1 mark

How many packets of crisps did Ed sell in total?

[   ] packets

1 mark

SECTION SIX — HANDLING DATA

Tables and Charts 1

(3) Ann counted the number of tickets sold for each ride at the funfair.

She put her data into a table and a pictogram.

Ride	Number of tickets
Bumper Cars	16
Ferris Wheel	
	18
Ghost train	15

Pictogram to show number of tickets sold

Bumper Cars

Ferris Wheel ⊕ ⊕ ⊕ ◁

Waltzer ⊕ ⊕ ⊕

Rollercoaster ⊕ ⊕ ⊕ ⊕ ⊟

Ghost Train

Number of tickets

⊕ = 4 tickets

Use the pictogram to fill in the gaps in the table.

1 mark

Complete the pictogram for the ghost train and bumper cars.

1 mark

Find the total number of tickets sold.

[_____ tickets]

1 mark

Use the information in the table and pictogram to complete the bar chart.

Number of tickets sold (y-axis: 0, 2, 4, 6, 8, 10, 12, 14, 16, 18, 20)

Ride (x-axis: Bumper Cars, Ferris Wheel, Waltzer, Roller-coaster, Ghost Train)

1 mark

Learning Objective:

"I can show information in a bar chart or a pictogram."

SECTION SIX — HANDLING DATA

Tables and Charts 2

1 Josie measures the height of a bamboo plant over 7 weeks.

She records the data in a table and plots a line graph.

Week	Height of bamboo (cm)
1	2
2	3
3	5
4	8
5	12
6	16
7	20

Graph to show height of bamboo

Height of bamboo (cm)

Fill in the three missing labels on the graph.

1 mark

How many centimetres did the bamboo grow between week 1 and week 7?

cm

1 mark

2 Mr Clark's class take a Maths test which is out of 50 marks.

He groups the marks and records them in a table.

Mark	Number of pupils
1-10	4
11-20	7
21-30	12
31-40	16
41-50	8

Use the information in the table to complete the bar chart.

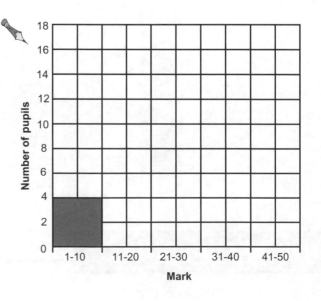

1 mark

Tables and Charts 2

3 Jack and Sam measure their height each year.

They record their results in a table.

Age	Jack's height (cm)	Sam's height (cm)
12	140	155
13	145	160
14	150	165
15	152	170
16	155	175

Use the information in the table to plot Sam's height on the line graph.

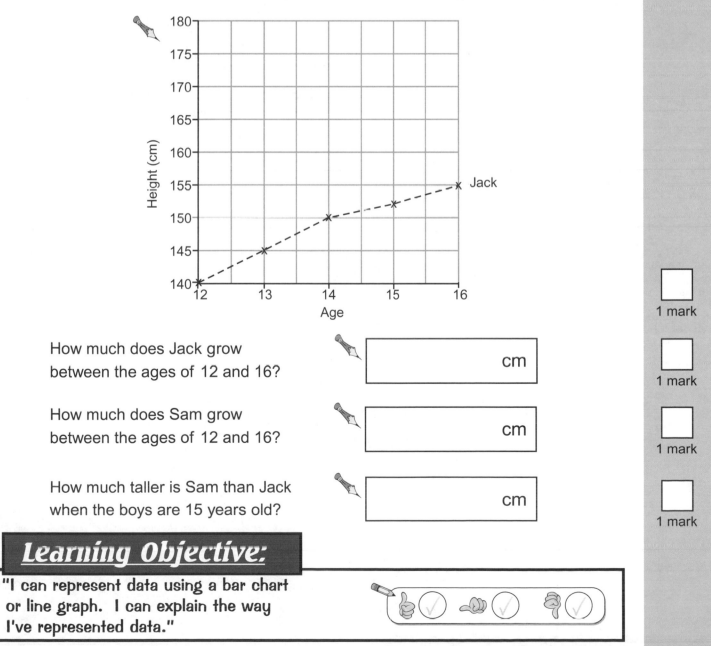

1 mark

How much does Jack grow
between the ages of 12 and 16?

cm

1 mark

How much does Sam grow
between the ages of 12 and 16?

cm

1 mark

How much taller is Sam than Jack
when the boys are 15 years old?

cm

1 mark

Learning Objective:

"I can represent data using a bar chart
or line graph. I can explain the way
I've represented data."

Number Patterns 1

(1) Shade in all the squares on this number grid that contain a number that is both a multiple of 2 and a multiple of 7.

1	2	3	4	5	6	7	8	9	10
11	12	13	14	15	16	17	18	19	20
21	22	23	24	25	26	27	28	29	30
31	32	33	34	35	36	37	38	39	40
41	42	43	44	45	46	47	48	49	50

1 mark

(2) Here is a repeating pattern of numbered shapes.

Write the number of the next two triangles in this pattern.

☐ and ☐

1 mark

(3) Circle the numbers that are factors of 40.

   2   6   8   12   18

1 mark

(4) Here is a Venn diagram for sorting numbers.

One number is in the wrong place. Place a cross over the incorrect number.

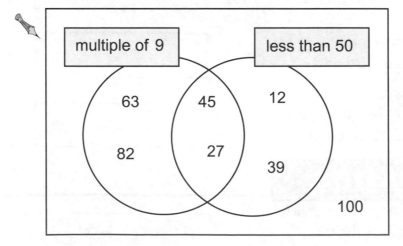

1 mark

Number Patterns 1

5 This sequence follows the rule:
'to get the next number, divide the last number by 2, then add 2'.
Write in the next 2 numbers.

84   44   24   [ ]   [ ]

1 mark

6 Write the missing number in the sequence below.

2   6   18   54   [ ]

1 mark

Explain how you worked it out.

[ ]

1 mark

7 This is a sequence of square numbers. They are ordered from smallest to largest. Fill in the missing numbers.

25   [ ]   49   64   [ ]   100

1 mark

8 Here is a sequence of numbers.

729   243   81   27

Describe the rule that links this sequence of numbers.

[ ]

1 mark

Learning Objective:

"I can see number patterns and can explain how the pattern works."

Number Patterns 2

1 Complete the addition when $x = 4$.

$$4x \quad + \quad 6 \quad = \quad \boxed{}$$

☐ 1 mark

2 In this sequence, the next number is made by doubling the last number. Complete the sequence.

8   **16** $\boxed{}$ $\boxed{}$ $\boxed{}$

☐ 1 mark

3 Find the value of $3z - 14$ when $z = 12$.

$\boxed{}$

☐ 1 mark

4 Here is a sequence of shaded shapes drawn on a grid.

The first three shapes have been drawn. Draw the fourth shape in the sequence.

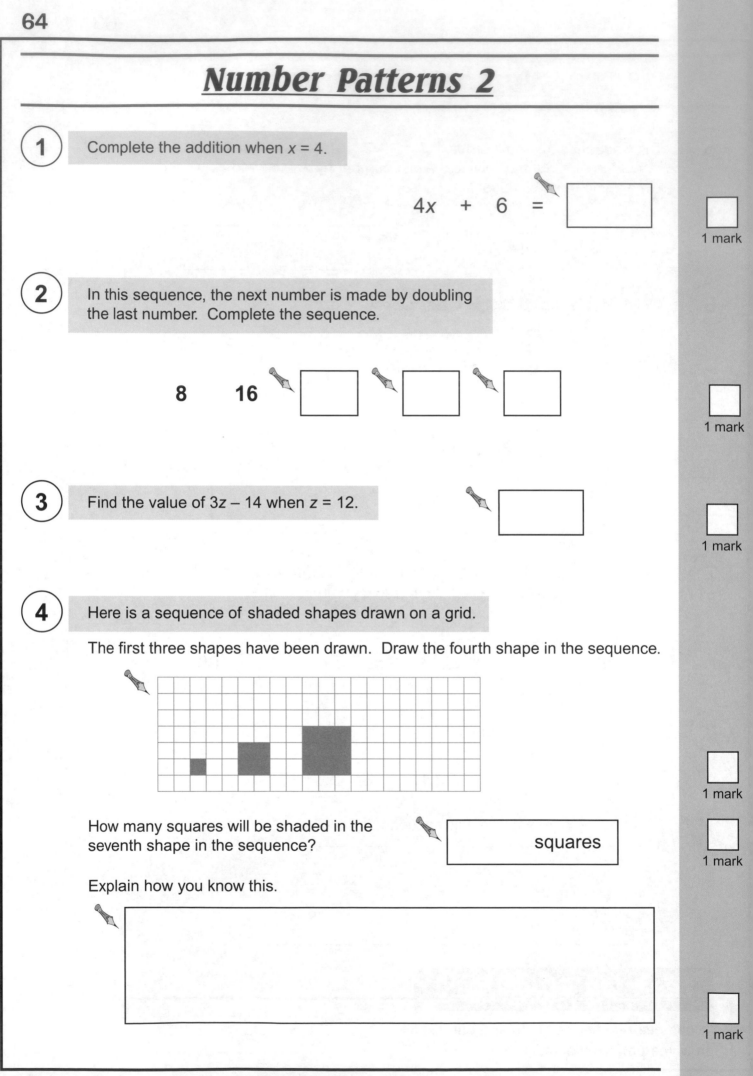

☐ 1 mark

How many squares will be shaded in the seventh shape in the sequence?

$\boxed{}$ squares

☐ 1 mark

Explain how you know this.

$\boxed{}$

☐ 1 mark

Number Patterns 2

5 Richard writes a number sequence. The rule is 'double the last number, then add 5'. The sequence contains the number 187. Work out the number before it in the sequence. Show your working.

2 marks

6 The rule for the sequence below is 'add ⭐'.

2.4 ☐ ☐ ☐ 17.2

What is the value of ⭐?
Show your working.

⭐ =

2 marks

Now fill in the missing numbers in the sequence above.

1 mark

7 Pete needs to buy 30 knives and 30 forks.

🔪 is the cost of 1 knife.   🍴 is the cost of 1 fork.

How much does Pete need to spend? Circle the correct answer.

30🔪 + 30🍴   30🔪 × 30🍴   30🔪🍴

1 mark

Learning Objective:

"I can describe and explain patterns, sequences and relationships."

👍 ✓   🤷 ✓   👎 ✓

SECTION SEVEN — USING AND APPLYING MATHEMATICS

Practice Test 3 — Levels 4c and 4b

1 Fill in the empty box below.

450   480

1 mark

2 Complete this subtraction.

342 – 278 =

1 mark

3 Fill in the empty box.

7600 ÷   = 76

1 mark

4 Complete the table below.

Shape	Faces	Vertices
Cube	6	
Triangular prism		6
Square-based pyramid	5	

2 marks

5 Write the missing numbers in the sequence below.

2   8   32

1 mark

Explain the rule that links the sequence of numbers.

1 mark

6 The grid below is made up of squares with sides of 1 cm.
Draw a rectangle with an area of 12 centimetres squared.

1 mark

7 In a school shop there are some boxes of crisps.
Each box contains 36 packets of crisps.

There are:

5 boxes of cheese and onion flavour

4 boxes of beef flavour

7 boxes of chicken flavour

How many packets of crisps are there altogether? Show your working.

packets

2 marks

8 Using a protractor, accurately measure the angle below.

°

1 mark

9 A restaurant sells 3 types of pizza.
The chart shows how many of each were sold on Saturday.

The restaurant sold 12 salami pizzas on Friday.
How many more salami pizzas did it sell on Saturday than on Friday?

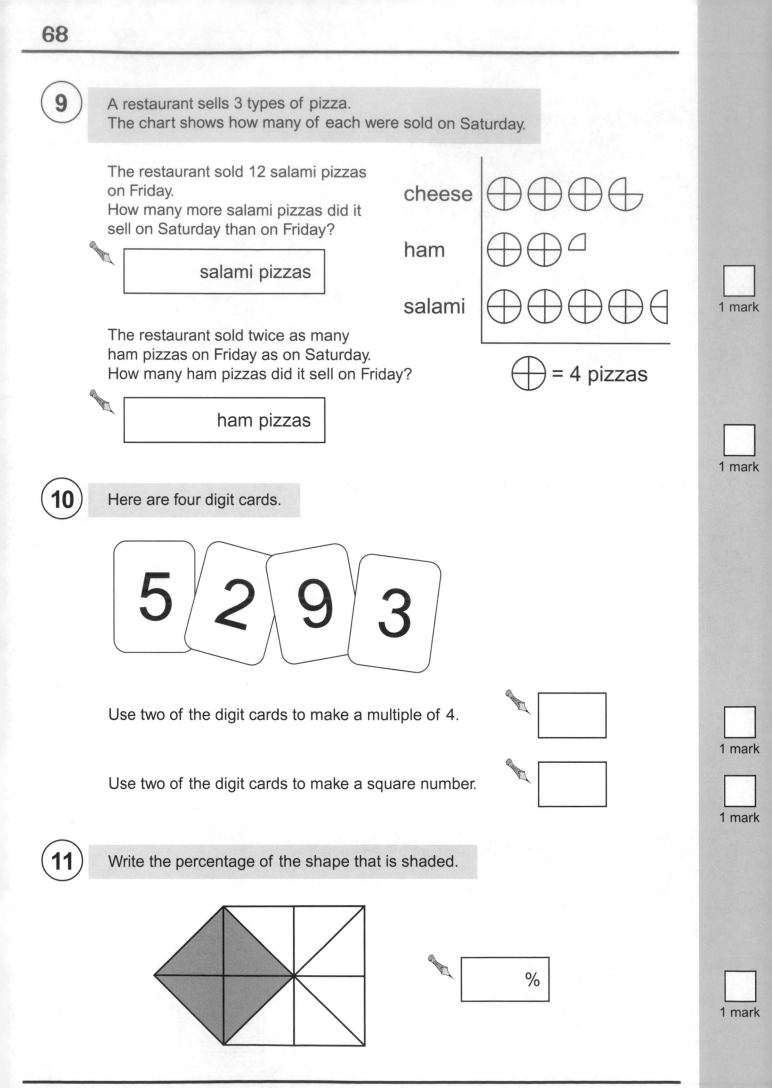

| salami pizzas |

The restaurant sold twice as many ham pizzas on Friday as on Saturday.
How many ham pizzas did it sell on Friday?

| ham pizzas |

cheese

ham

salami

$\bigoplus$ = 4 pizzas

1 mark

1 mark

10 Here are four digit cards.

5 2 9 3

Use two of the digit cards to make a multiple of 4.

1 mark

Use two of the digit cards to make a square number.

1 mark

11 Write the percentage of the shape that is shaded.

%

1 mark

12 Using a protractor, accurately measure the obtuse angle in this shape.

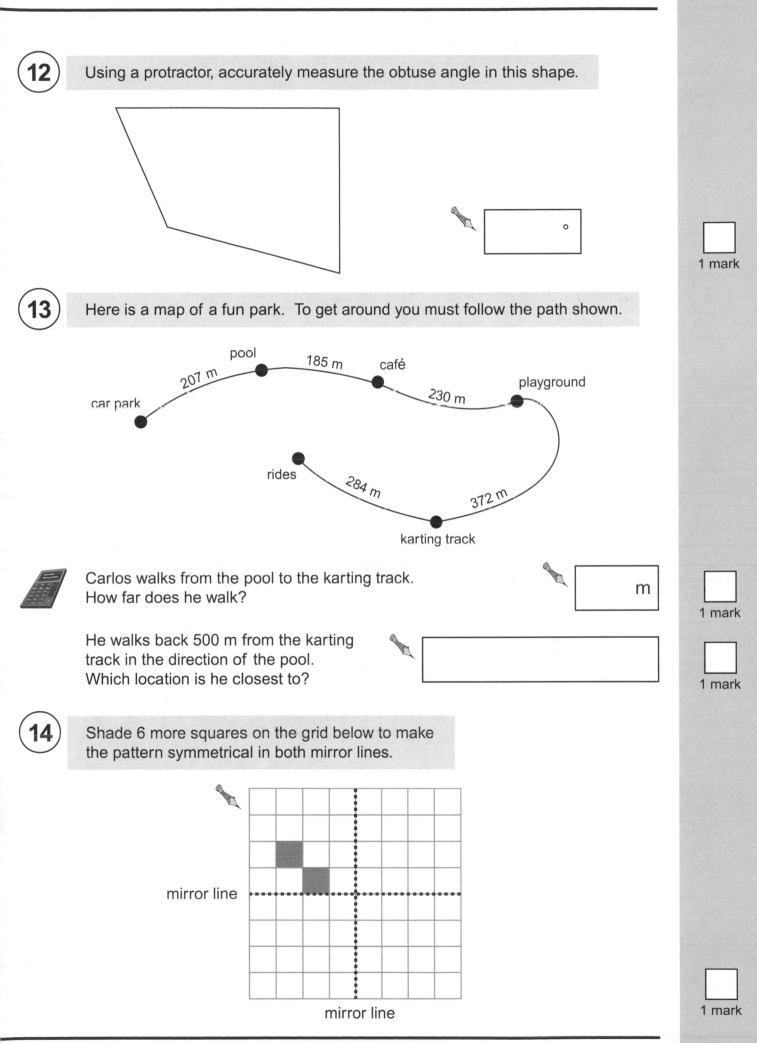

1 mark

13 Here is a map of a fun park. To get around you must follow the path shown.

Carlos walks from the pool to the karting track.
How far does he walk?

m

1 mark

He walks back 500 m from the karting
track in the direction of the pool.
Which location is he closest to?

1 mark

14 Shade 6 more squares on the grid below to make
the pattern symmetrical in both mirror lines.

mirror line

mirror line

1 mark

Practice Test 4 — Levels 4B and 4A

1 Calculate 36.7 × 4.

1 mark

2 Shade in 20% of the squares that make up this grid.

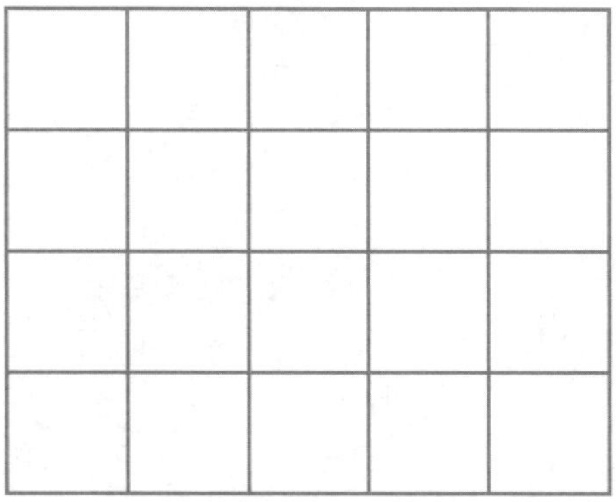

1 mark

3 The rule for the sequence below is 'add ⬡'.

7.8 [ ] [ ] [ ] **9.4**

What is the value of ⬡?
Show your working.

⬡ =

2 marks

4 Calculate 204 ÷ 6.

1 mark

5 Mark chooses a number.
He multiplies it by 3 then subtracts 12. The answer is 21.
What number did Mark choose?

1 mark

6 Write the coordinates for point S.

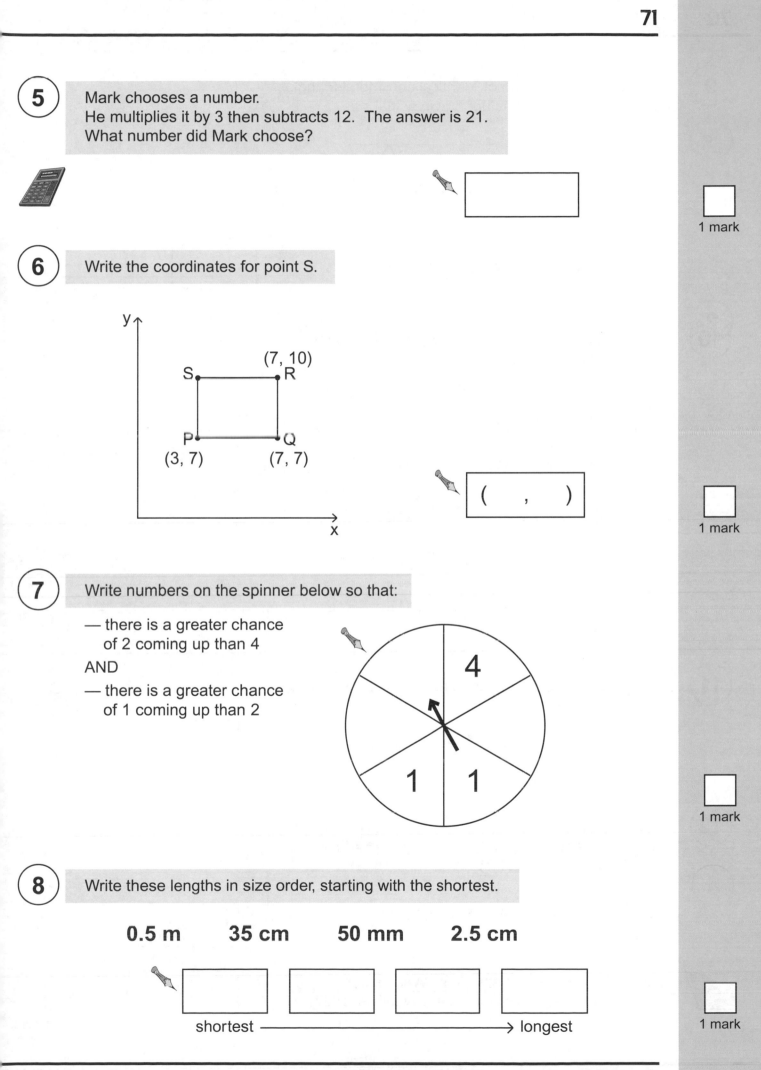

(,)

1 mark

7 Write numbers on the spinner below so that:

— there is a greater chance
of 2 coming up than 4

AND

— there is a greater chance
of 1 coming up than 2

1 mark

8 Write these lengths in size order, starting with the shortest.

0.5 m   **35 cm**   **50 mm**   **2.5 cm**

shortest ───────────────────────→ longest

1 mark

9 This shape is made up of identical equilateral triangles with sides of 4 cm. It is not drawn actual size.

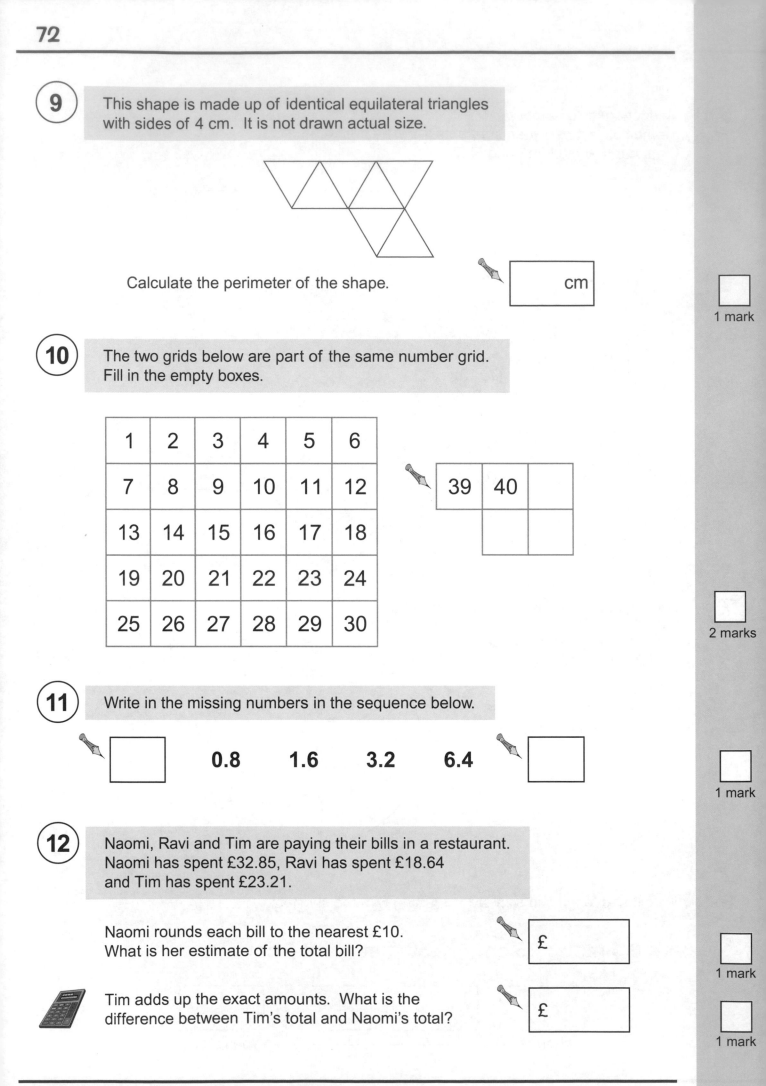

Calculate the perimeter of the shape.

| cm |

1 mark

10 The two grids below are part of the same number grid. Fill in the empty boxes.

1	2	3	4	5	6
7	8	9	10	11	12
13	14	15	16	17	18
19	20	21	22	23	24
25	26	27	28	29	30

39	40	

2 marks

11 Write in the missing numbers in the sequence below.

| | **0.8**   **1.6**   **3.2**   **6.4** | |

1 mark

12 Naomi, Ravi and Tim are paying their bills in a restaurant. Naomi has spent £32.85, Ravi has spent £18.64 and Tim has spent £23.21.

Naomi rounds each bill to the nearest £10. What is her estimate of the total bill?

£ |

1 mark

Tim adds up the exact amounts. What is the difference between Tim's total and Naomi's total?

£ |

1 mark

13 Below is a pie chart showing favourite pets in a class of 24 children.

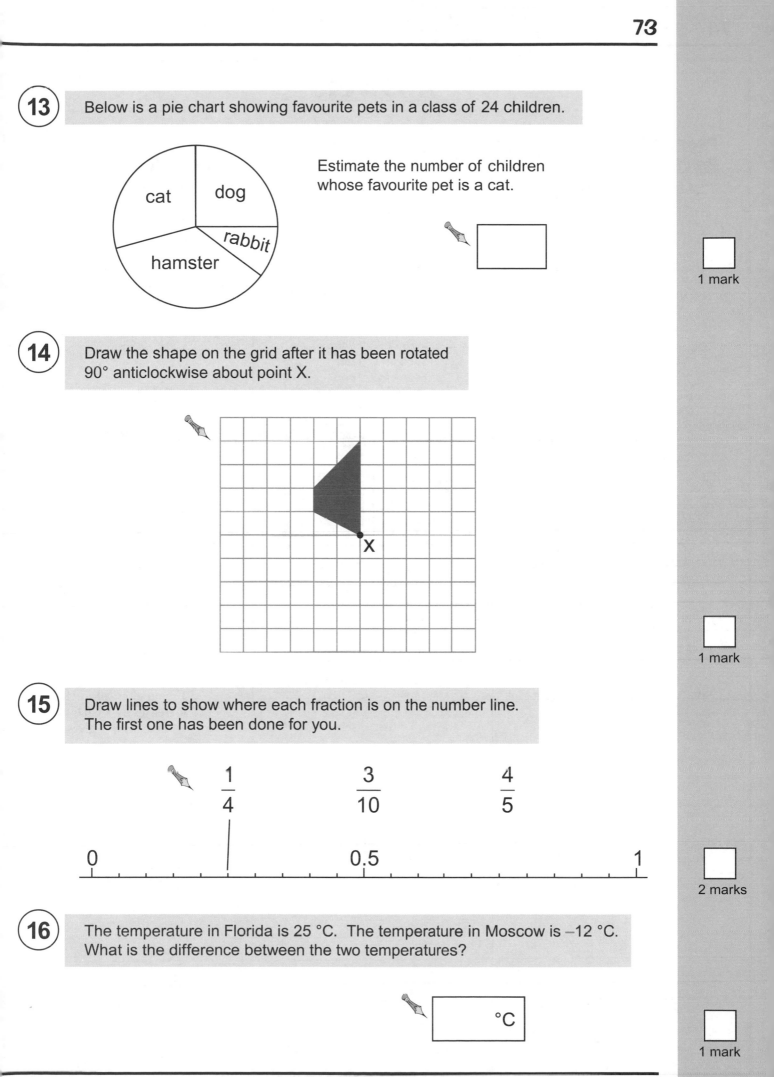

Estimate the number of children whose favourite pet is a cat.

1 mark

14 Draw the shape on the grid after it has been rotated 90° anticlockwise about point X.

X

1 mark

15 Draw lines to show where each fraction is on the number line. The first one has been done for you.

$\dfrac{1}{4}$ $\dfrac{3}{10}$ $\dfrac{4}{5}$

0   0.5   1

2 marks

16 The temperature in Florida is 25 °C. The temperature in Moscow is –12 °C. What is the difference between the two temperatures?

°C

1 mark

Answers

Pages 2-5 — Practice Test 1 — Levels 3B and 3A

Q1 4 × 60 = 240
4 × 5 = 20
240 + 20 = 260
4 peaches cost **260p** (£2.60)
(1 mark)

Q2
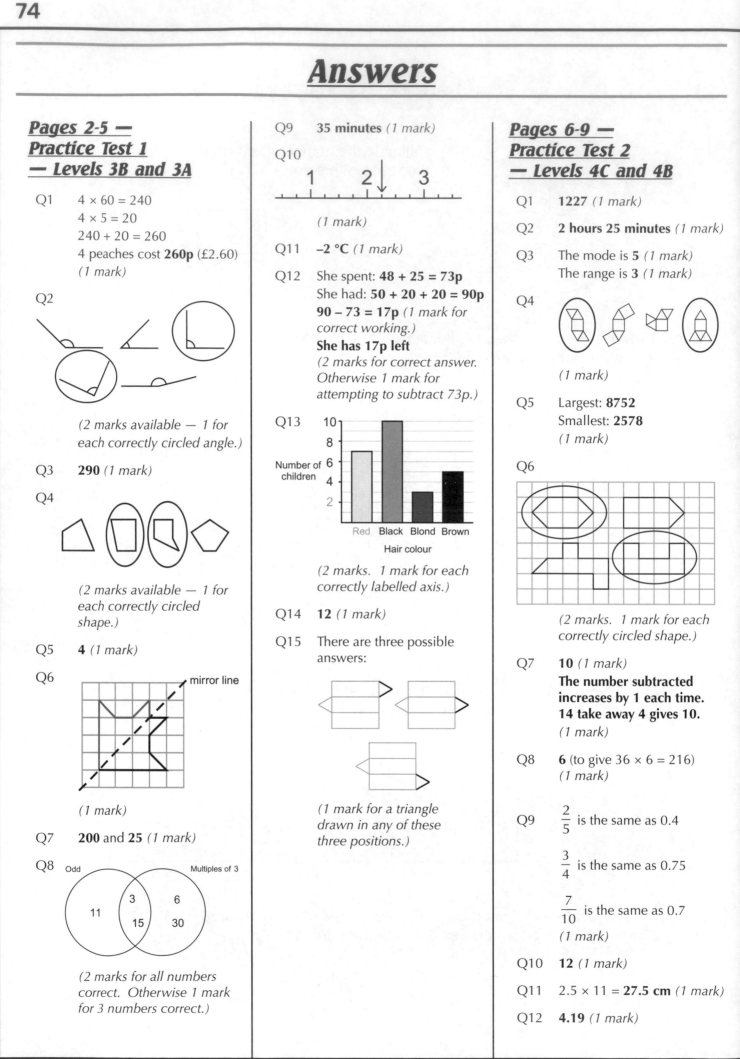
(2 marks available — 1 for each correctly circled angle.)

Q3 **290** *(1 mark)*

Q4
(2 marks available — 1 for each correctly circled shape.)

Q5 **4** *(1 mark)*

Q6
mirror line
(1 mark)

Q7 **200** and **25** *(1 mark)*

Q8
Odd   Multiples of 3

11   3   6
       15   30

(2 marks for all numbers correct. Otherwise 1 mark for 3 numbers correct.)

Q9 **35 minutes** *(1 mark)*

Q10
1   2   ↓   3
(1 mark)

Q11 **–2 °C** *(1 mark)*

Q12 She spent: **48 + 25 = 73p**
She had: **50 + 20 + 20 = 90p**
90 – 73 = 17p *(1 mark for correct working.)*
She has 17p left
(2 marks for correct answer. Otherwise 1 mark for attempting to subtract 73p.)

Q13
Number of children (10, 8, 6, 4, 2)
Red Black Blond Brown
Hair colour
(2 marks. 1 mark for each correctly labelled axis.)

Q14 **12** *(1 mark)*

Q15 There are three possible answers:
(1 mark for a triangle drawn in any of these three positions.)

Pages 6-9 — Practice Test 2 — Levels 4C and 4B

Q1 **1227** *(1 mark)*

Q2 **2 hours 25 minutes** *(1 mark)*

Q3 The mode is **5** *(1 mark)*
The range is **3** *(1 mark)*

Q4
(1 mark)

Q5 Largest: **8752**
Smallest: **2578**
(1 mark)

Q6
(2 marks. 1 mark for each correctly circled shape.)

Q7 **10** *(1 mark)*
The number subtracted increases by 1 each time. 14 take away 4 gives 10.
(1 mark)

Q8 **6** (to give 36 × 6 = 216)
(1 mark)

Q9 $\frac{2}{5}$ is the same as 0.4
$\frac{3}{4}$ is the same as 0.75
$\frac{7}{10}$ is the same as 0.7
(1 mark)

Q10 **12** *(1 mark)*

Q11 2.5 × 11 = **27.5 cm** *(1 mark)*

Q12 **4.19** *(1 mark)*

Answers

Q13

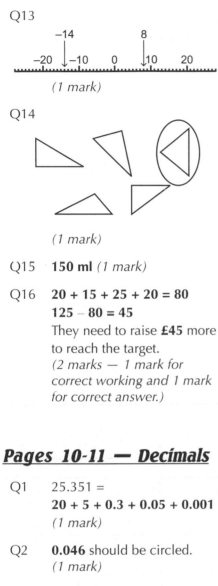

(1 mark)

Q14

(1 mark)

Q15 **150 ml** *(1 mark)*

Q16 **20 + 15 + 25 + 20 = 80**
125 – 80 = 45
They need to raise **£45** more to reach the target.
(2 marks — 1 mark for correct working and 1 mark for correct answer.)

Pages 10-11 — Decimals

Q1 25.351 =
20 + 5 + 0.3 + 0.05 + 0.001
(1 mark)

Q2 **0.046** should be circled.
(1 mark)

Q3 From left to right:
3.17, 3.24
(2 marks. 1 mark for each correct number)

Q4 From smallest to largest:
1.505, 1.925, 1.975, 2.035, 2.180 *(1 mark)*

Q5 **0.81** *(1 mark)*

Q6 From left to right:
6.143, 6.155
(2 marks. 1 mark for each correct number)

Q7 From largest to smallest:
0.918, 0.908, 0.484, 0.397, 0.392 *(1 mark)*

Q8 0.98 rounds to **1**
6.49 rounds to **6**
13.732 rounds to **14**
9.199 rounds to **9**
(2 marks for all answers correct. Otherwise 1 mark for 3 correct answers.)

Pages 12-13 — Numbers and Number Lines

Q1 **–7, 6** and **23**
(2 marks for all 3 correct. Otherwise 1 mark for any 2 correct.)

Q2 Number line may look like:

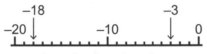

Counting between the two gives the answer:
15 °C difference in temperature
(2 marks for correct answer and number line. Otherwise 1 mark for either correct answer or correct attempt at number line.)

Q3 **>** and **>**
(2 marks — 1 mark for each symbol.)

Q4 Number line may look like:

Use the number line to count back to:
–4 °C
(2 marks for correct answer and number line. Otherwise 1 mark for either correct answer or correct attempt at number line.)

Q5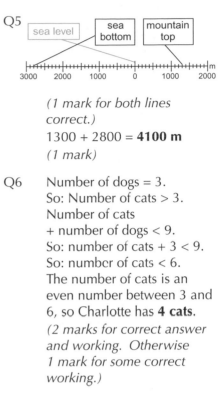
(1 mark for both lines correct.)
1300 + 2800 = **4100 m**
(1 mark)

Q6 Number of dogs = 3.
So: Number of cats > 3.
Number of cats
+ number of dogs < 9.
So: number of cats + 3 < 9.
So: number of cats < 6.
The number of cats is an even number between 3 and 6, so Charlotte has **4 cats**.
(2 marks for correct answer and working. Otherwise 1 mark for some correct working.)

Q7 **6** *(1 mark)*
24 *(1 mark)*

Pages 14-15 —Percentages

Q1 From left to right:
85%, 30%
(1 mark)

Q2 4 squares should be shaded. E.g.

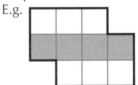

(1 mark)

$\frac{40}{100}$ or $\frac{4}{10}$ or $\frac{2}{5}$ *(1 mark)*

Q3 $\frac{3}{10} = \frac{30}{100} = 30\%$
$100\% - 30\% = 70\%$
She has **70%** left to read.
(1 mark)

Answers

Q4 **74**% and $\frac{4}{6}$ should be circled.
(1 mark for both correct amounts.)

Q5 From top to bottom:
50% should be circled *(1 mark)*
75% should be circled *(1 mark)*

Q6 $\frac{3}{4} = 75\%$

$\frac{8}{10} = 80\%$

80% − 75% = **5**%
(2 marks for correct answer. Otherwise 1 mark for converting fractions into percentages.)

Pages 16-17
—Proportion and Ratio

Q1 **£1.75** *(1 mark)*

Q2 **45p** *(1 mark)*

Q3 **7 lengths** *(1 mark)*

Q4 **£42** *(1 mark)*

Q5 Number of pupils in 1 team
= 32 ÷ 8 = 4
Number of pupils in 5 teams
= 4 × 5 = **20 pupils**
(2 marks for correct answer. Otherwise 1 mark for 32 ÷ 8 = 4.)

Q6 6 potatoes is 3 times as many as 2. James will have:
3 × 3 = **9 carrots** *(1 mark)*
4 potatoes is twice as many as 2. Mila will have:
2 × 7 = **14 green beans** *(1 mark)*

Q7 42 ÷ 7 = 6
2 × 6 = **12 pigs**
(2 marks for correct answer. Otherwise 1 mark for 42 ÷ 7 = 6.)

Q8 Number of eggs in 1 box
= 24 ÷ 4 = 6
Number of boxes
= total number of eggs ÷ number of eggs in 1 box
= 54 ÷ 6 = **9 boxes**.
(2 marks for correct answer. Otherwise 1 mark for 24 ÷ 4 = 6.)

Pages 18-19
— Checking Calculations

Q1 Smallest: **425** *(1 mark)*
Biggest: **434** *(1 mark)*

Q2 **43** *(1 mark)*

Q3 **1238 + 794 = 2032** or **794 + 1238 = 2032**
Yes, Jim is right.
(1 mark for both parts correct.)

Q4 Estimate the correct answer using **140 ÷ 10 = 14**.
6 is much smaller than 14.
Or: **6 × 9 = 54. 54 is much smaller than 114.**
(1 mark)

Q5 Any two of:
91 ÷ 13 = 7
13 × 7 = 91
7 × 13 = 91
(2 marks. 1 mark for each correct answer.)

Q6 7.2 − 2.9 can be rounded to 7 − 3 = **4** *(1 mark)*

Q7 12.3 × 9.8 can be estimated as 12 × 10 = 120.
120 should be circled.
(1 mark)

Q8 £2.00 + £1.00 + 50p = **£3.50** *(1 mark)*
Lower — all prices were rounded down when estimating. *(1 mark)*

Pages 20-21
—Factors and Multiples

Q1 **False** *(1 mark)*
True *(1 mark)*
All the numbers in circles are even. Square numbers can be odd, e.g. 9. *(1 mark)*

Q2 multiple of 6:
24, **42** or **72** *(1 mark)*
factor of 54: **27** *(1 mark)*

Q3 **16** and **24** should be circled. *(1 mark)*

Q4 **1 × 32, 2 × 16, 4 × 8** *(1 mark)*

Q5 Many possible answers, e.g.

	multiple of 7	not a multiple of 7
even	14	22
not even	21	11

(2 marks for all answers correct. Otherwise 1 mark for 3 correct answers.)

Q6 **NO** should be circled.
Many possible examples, e.g.
8 × 5 = 40 or **8 × 10 = 80**
(1 mark for correct answer and example. Accept any multiple of 8 ending 0.)

Q7 E.g. **24, 48, 72** or any other common multiple. *(1 mark)*

Q8 **21, 25** *(1 mark)*
NO should be circled.
84 is an even number and there will be no even numbers in the sequence because it starts on an odd number.
(1 mark for correct answer and explanation.)

Answers

Pages 22-23 — Multiplication and Division

Q1 **3** and **7** should be circled. *(1 mark for both numbers correct.)*

Q2 **27**, **36** and **54** should be circled. *(1 mark for all 3 numbers correct.)*

Q3 **4 × 7 = 28**
28 ÷ 7 = 4 or 28 ÷ 4 = 7
(1 mark for both parts correct.)

Q4 28 ÷ 7 = **4** *(1 mark)*
40 × 8 = **320** *(1 mark)*
54 ÷ 9 = **6** *(1 mark)*

Q5 Multiple of 9:
27 or **72** *(1 mark)*
Multiple of 8:
24, **64** or **72** *(1 mark)*

Q6 9 – 2 = 7
7 × 6 = **42** *(1 mark)*

Q7 Number of boxes in each pack = 6 + 1 = 7
56 ÷ 7 = **8 packs** *(1 mark)*

Q8 84 – 3 = 81
81 ÷ 9 = **9 friends** *(1 mark)*

Pages 24-25 — Square Numbers

Q1 7 × 7 = **49** *(1 mark)*

Q2 **FALSE** should be circled. Any even number squared will be a multiple of 4, e.g.
2 × 2 = 4 = 1 × 4
6 × 6 = 36 = 9 × 4
8 × 8 = 64 = 16 × 4 etc.
(1 mark for correct answer and example.)

Q3 60 × 60 = 6 × 10 × 6 × 10
= 6 × 6 × 10 × 10
= 36 × 100 **3600**
(2 marks for correct answer. Otherwise 1 mark for 6 × 6 = 36.)

Q4 Many possible answers, e.g.

	square number	not a square number
multiple of 3	9	12
not a multiple of 3	16	22

(2 marks for all answers correct. Otherwise 1 mark for 3 correct answers.)

Q5 **25** *(1 mark)*

Q6 **25**, **64** and **121** should be circled.
(1 mark for all three numbers correct.)

Q7 **NO** should be circled.
(1 mark)
$8^2 = 64$ and $9^2 = 81$. There cannot be any square numbers in between.
(1 mark for correct explanation.)

Q8 **1** and **9** *(1 mark)*
9 and **16** *(1 mark)*

Pages 26-27 — Multiply and Divide by 10 and 100

Q1 75 × 100 = **7500** *(1 mark)*

Q2 160 ÷ 10 = **16** *(1 mark)*

Q3 5300 ÷ **53** = 100 *(1 mark)*

Q4 A: **114**
B: **800**
C: **550**
D: **400**
(2 marks for all 4 correct. Otherwise 1 mark for 2 or 3 correct.)

Q5 45.3 × 10 = **453** *(1 mark)*

Q6 4.6 × **100** = 460 *(1 mark)*

Q7 863 ÷ 100 = **8.63** *(1 mark)*

Q8 **C** £120
D £1200
B £12
(2 marks for all 3 correct. Otherwise 1 mark for 1 or 2 correct.)

Pages 28-29 — Mental Maths

Q1 **60** *(1 mark)*

Q2 **62p** *(1 mark)*

Q3 **37 badges** *(1 mark)*

Q4 **41** *(1 mark)*

Q5 **48** *(1 mark)*

Q6 **121** *(1 mark)*

Q7 **14** *(1 mark)*

Q8 an apple and a bunch of cherries cost **90p** *(1 mark)*
a banana and a bunch of cherries cost **112p** or **£1.12** *(1 mark)*
a banana and two apples cost **103p** or **£1.03** *(1 mark)*

Q9 **67** *(1 mark)*

Pages 30-31 — Written Adding and Subtracting 1

Q1 224 – 58 = **166** *(1 mark)*

Q2 36 + 47 = **£83** *(1 mark)*

Q3 585 + 367 = 952 *(1 mark)*
439 + 316 = 755 *(1 mark)*

Q4 **48 cm** *(1 mark)*
91 cm *(1 mark)*

Q5 909 – 212 = **697** *(1 mark)*

Q6 **£3.85** *(1 mark)*

Q7 **£3.95** *(1 mark)*
£1.05 *(1 mark)*

Answers

Pages 32-33 — Written Adding and Subtracting 2

Q1 **1803** *(1 mark)*

Q2 **12.5 and 37.5**
25.2 and 50.2
52 and 77
(2 marks for all correct pairs. Otherwise 1 mark for 1 or 2 correct pairs.)

Q3 **59.7 m** *(1 mark)*

Q4 **Flower A: 36.7 cm** *(1 mark)*
Flower B: 88 cm *(1 mark)*

Q5 54.2 – 37 = 17.2
17.2 – <u>0.8</u> = 16.4
So the missing digit is **8**
(1 mark)

Q6 5.39 + 8.46 = **13.85**
(1 mark)

Q7 **12.05** *(1 mark)*
10.82 *(1 mark)*

Q8 9 + 7 = 16
0.24 + 0.21 = 0.45
16 + 0.45 = 16.45
So **9.24 and 7.21** should be circled. *(1 mark)*

Pages 34-35 — Written Multiplying and Dividing

Q1 **1435** *(1 mark)*

Q2 **1225 g** *(1 mark)*

Q3 **£2.80** *(1 mark)*
£11.20 *(1 mark)*

Q4 **85 g** *(1 mark)*

Q5 **56** *(1 mark)*

Q6 **29.1** *(1 mark)*

Q7 **£5.64** *(1 mark)*
£8.93 *(1 mark)*

Q8 **2, 6** *(1 mark)*

Pages 36-37 — Calculators

Q1 **£43.20** *(1 mark)*

Q2 **7**
(Upper row digit — 1 mark)
8
(Lower row digit — 1 mark)

Q3 **–6.2** *(1 mark)*

Q4 **135** *(1 mark)*

Q5 **4 g** *(1 mark)*

Q6 **136 cm** *(1 mark)*

Q7 **£7.50** *(1 mark)*

Pages 38-39 — 2D Shapes

Q1
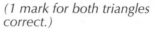
(1 mark for both triangles correct.)

Q2 E.g.
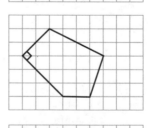

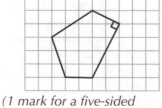
(1 mark for a five-sided shape with one right angle.)

Q3
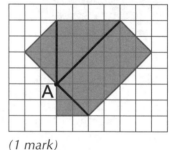
(1 mark. Both lines must be correct.)

Q4 E.g.

(1 mark)

E.g.
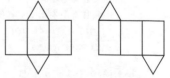
(1 mark)

Q5

(1 mark)

Q6 **True**
False
True
(1 mark for all three answers correct.)

Pages 40-41 — 3D Shapes

Q1 **6 edges** *(1 mark)*

Q2 **9 faces** *(1 mark)*

Q3 There are many ways to draw the net for this prism. E.g.

The triangles should be equilateral, and all three rectangles should be the same size.
(1 mark)

Answers

Q4

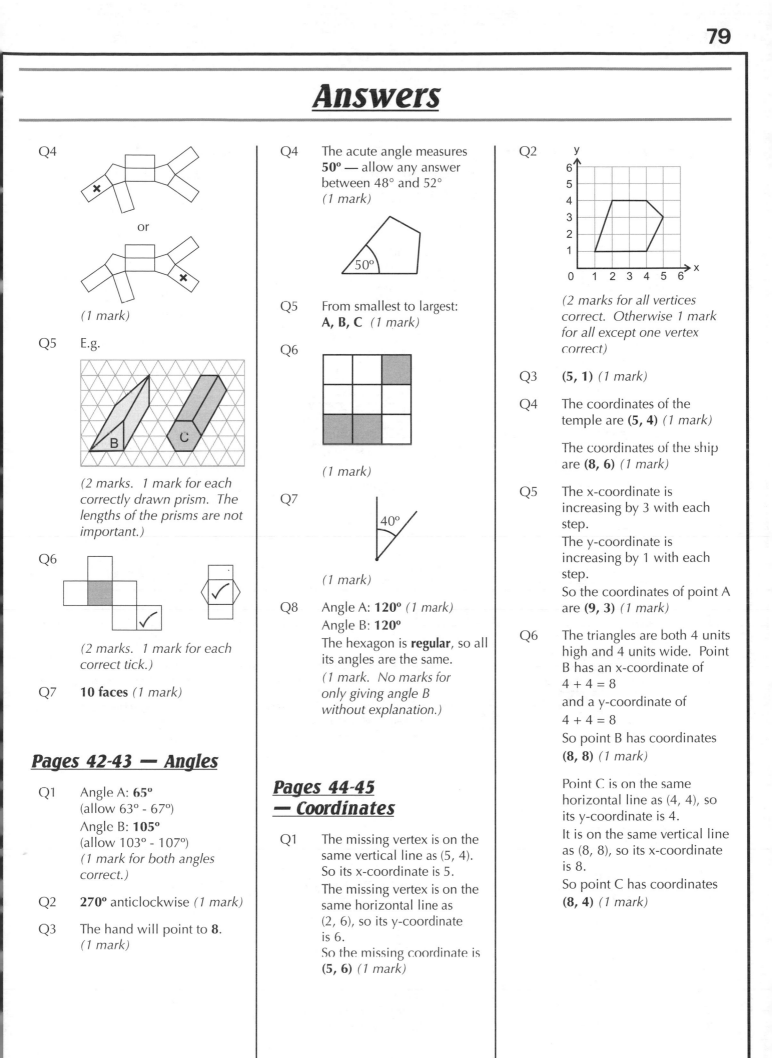

(1 mark)

Q5 E.g.

(2 marks. 1 mark for each correctly drawn prism. The lengths of the prisms are not important.)

Q6

(2 marks. 1 mark for each correct tick.)

Q7 **10 faces** *(1 mark)*

Pages 42-43 — Angles

Q1 Angle A: **65°**
(allow 63° - 67°)
Angle B: **105°**
(allow 103° - 107°)
(1 mark for both angles correct.)

Q2 **270°** anticlockwise *(1 mark)*

Q3 The hand will point to **8**.
(1 mark)

Q4 The acute angle measures **50°** — allow any answer between 48° and 52°
(1 mark)

Q5 From smallest to largest:
A, B, C *(1 mark)*

Q6

(1 mark)

Q7

40°

(1 mark)

Q8 Angle A: **120°** *(1 mark)*
Angle B: **120°**
The hexagon is **regular**, so all its angles are the same.
(1 mark. No marks for only giving angle B without explanation.)

Pages 44-45 — Coordinates

Q1 The missing vertex is on the same vertical line as (5, 4). So its x-coordinate is 5.
The missing vertex is on the same horizontal line as (2, 6), so its y-coordinate is 6.
So the missing coordinate is **(5, 6)** *(1 mark)*

Q2

(2 marks for all vertices correct. Otherwise 1 mark for all except one vertex correct)

Q3 **(5, 1)** *(1 mark)*

Q4 The coordinates of the temple are **(5, 4)** *(1 mark)*

The coordinates of the ship are **(8, 6)** *(1 mark)*

Q5 The x-coordinate is increasing by 3 with each step.
The y-coordinate is increasing by 1 with each step.
So the coordinates of point A are **(9, 3)** *(1 mark)*

Q6 The triangles are both 4 units high and 4 units wide. Point B has an x-coordinate of $4 + 4 = 8$
and a y-coordinate of $4 + 4 = 8$
So point B has coordinates **(8, 8)** *(1 mark)*

Point C is on the same horizontal line as (4, 4), so its y-coordinate is 4.
It is on the same vertical line as (8, 8), so its x-coordinate is 8.
So point C has coordinates **(8, 4)** *(1 mark)*

Answers

Pages 46-47 — Symmetry

Q1 **A** and **C**
(2 marks. 1 mark for each correct letter.)

Q2 A square has **4** lines of symmetry *(1 mark)*

A regular pentagon has **5** lines of symmetry *(1 mark)*

Q3
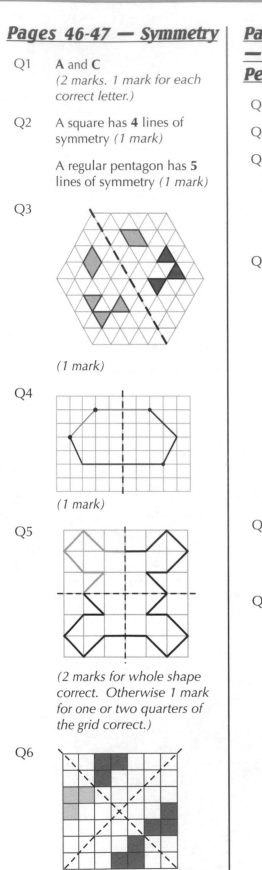

(1 mark)

Q4

(1 mark)

Q5

(2 marks for whole shape correct. Otherwise 1 mark for one or two quarters of the grid correct.)

Q6

(2 marks for all nine squares correct. Otherwise 1 mark for one or two quarters of the grid correct.)

Pages 48-49 — Calculating Perimeter and Area

Q1 $4 \times 8 =$ **32 cm** *(1 mark)*

Q2 **13 cm²** *(1 mark)*

Q3 E.g.
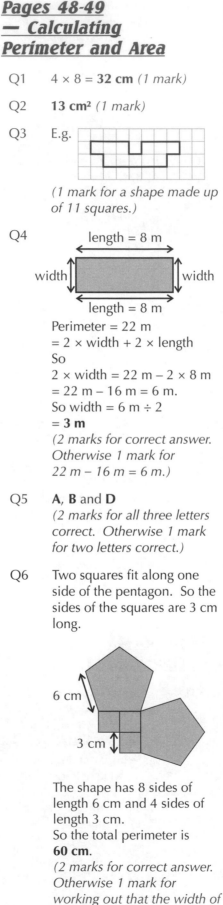

(1 mark for a shape made up of 11 squares.)

Q4

length = 8 m

width — width

length = 8 m

Perimeter = 22 m
= 2 × width + 2 × length
So
2 × width = 22 m – 2 × 8 m
= 22 m – 16 m = 6 m.
So width = 6 m ÷ 2
= **3 m**
(2 marks for correct answer. Otherwise 1 mark for 22 m – 16 m = 6 m.)

Q5 **A**, **B** and **D**
(2 marks for all three letters correct. Otherwise 1 mark for two letters correct.)

Q6 Two squares fit along one side of the pentagon. So the sides of the squares are 3 cm long.

6 cm

3 cm

The shape has 8 sides of length 6 cm and 4 sides of length 3 cm.
So the total perimeter is **60 cm**.
(2 marks for correct answer. Otherwise 1 mark for working out that the width of the squares is 3 cm.)

Pages 50-51 — Units and Measures

Q1 **4 m** should be circled *(1 mark)*
15 ml should be circled *(1 mark)*

Q2 **3700 ml**, **2.5 m**
(1 mark for each correct answer.)

Q3 The amount of water in the container starts at 450 ml.
450 ml – 250 ml = **200 ml**
(1 mark)

Q4 6 × 200 ml = 1200 ml
1.5 l = 1500 ml
1500 ml – 1200 ml
= **300 ml**
(2 marks for correct answer. Otherwise 1 mark for 6 × 200 ml = 1200 ml.)

Q5 The left edge of the coin is at 32 mm.
The right edge of the coin is at 50 mm.
The width of the coin is 50 mm – 32 mm = **18 mm**
(1 mark)

Q6 Sandwich 1: **230 g** *(1 mark)*
Sandwich 2: **370 g** *(1 mark)*

Total mass:
230 g + 370 g = 600 g
= **0.6 kg** *(1 mark)*

The arrow should be drawn like this:

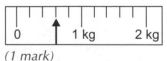

(1 mark)

Answers

Pages 52-53
— Analysing Data

Q1 **2** *(1 mark)*
blue *(1 mark)*

Q2 **422441**
124544
632544
444466
(2 marks for all correct answers. Otherwise 1 mark for 2 or more correct answers and no incorrect answers.)

Q3 **walking**
(1 mark)

Q4 **brown** *(1 mark)*

Q5 6 – 1 = **5** *(1 mark)*

Q6 **9** *(1 mark)*
12 – 2 = **10** *(1 mark)*

Q7 ½ + 3½ = **4 hours**
(2 marks for correct answer. Otherwise 1 mark for trying to add range to lowest value.)

Q8 **one film** *(1 mark)*

Pages 54-55
— Chance and Likelihood

Q1 **impossible** *(1 mark)*
likely *(1 mark)*

Q2 **winter** *(1 mark)*
Iceland *(1 mark)*

Q3 **less likely** *(1 mark)*
Maxine *(1 mark)*
Dennis *(1 mark)*

Q4 **certain** *(1 mark)*
impossible (1 mark)

Q5 **most** *(1 mark)*
middle *(1 mark)*
least *(1 mark)*

Q6 **star** *(1 mark)*
cross *(1 mark)*
Yes — there are an equal number of triangles and circles. *(1 mark)*

Pages 56-57 — Data

Q1
Animal	Tally	Frequency
Cat	Ⅲ Ⅰ	6
Dog	ⅠⅠⅠⅠ	4
Rabbit	ⅠⅠ	2

(1 mark)

There are **2** more dogs than rabbits. *(1 mark)*

Q2
Bird	Tally	Frequency
blackbird	ЖⅠ	6
crow	ЖⅠⅠⅠ	9
sparrow	ⅠⅠⅠⅠ	4
starling	ЖЖЖⅠ	16

(1 mark)

There were **35** birds in total. *(1 mark)*

Q3 The correct answer is **"What is your favourite sandwich filling?"**. *(1 mark)*

Q4
Colour	Number of cars
Blue	Ж ⅠⅠⅠ
Red	Ж Ж
Green	Ж ⅠⅠⅠ
Silver	Ж

(1 mark)

Q5
Number of sandwiches sold		
Day	Tally	Frequency
Monday	Ж Ж ⅠⅠⅠⅠ	14
Tuesday	Ж Ж Ж ⅠⅠ	17
Wednesday	Ж Ж Ж ⅠⅠⅠ	18
Thursday	Ж Ж Ж ⅠⅠ	17
Friday	Ж Ж ⅠⅠ	12

(1 mark)
He sold the most sandwiches on **Wednesday.** *(1 mark)*
He sold a total of **78** sandwiches. *(1 mark)*

Pages 58-59
— Tables and Charts 1

Q1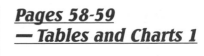

(1 mark)
20 + 14 + 9 + 16 = **59 fish**
(1 mark)

Q2 **ready salted** *(1 mark)*
11 packets *(1 mark)*
46 packets *(1 mark)*

Q3
Ride	Number of tickets
Bumper Cars	10
Ferris Wheel	13
Waltzer	11
Rollercoaster	18
Ghost Train	15

(1 mark)

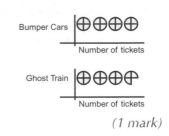

(1 mark)

73 tickets *(1 mark)*

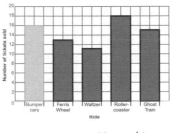

(1 mark)

Answers

Pages 60-61
—Tables and Charts 2

Q1

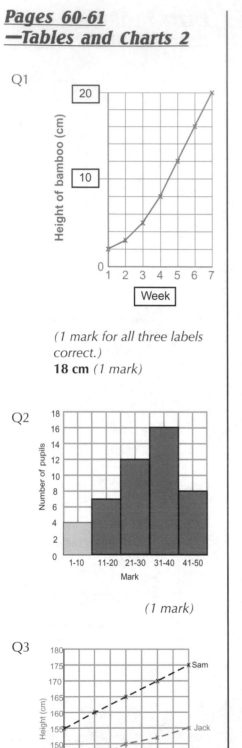

(1 mark for all three labels correct.)
18 cm *(1 mark)*

Q2

Q3

15 cm *(1 mark)*
20 cm *(1 mark)*
18 cm *(1 mark)*

Pages 62-63
— Number Patterns 1

Q1

1	2	3	4	5	6	7	8	9	10
11	12	13	14	15	16	17	18	19	20
21	22	23	24	25	26	27	28	29	30
31	32	33	34	35	36	37	38	39	40
41	42	43	44	45	46	47	48	49	50

(1 mark)

Q2　**28** and **38** *(1 mark)*

Q3　**2** and **8** *(1 mark)*

Q4　**82** is in the wrong place on the diagram. *(1 mark)*

Q5　**14** and **9** *(1 mark)*

Q6　**162** *(1 mark)*
The next number is three times the one before it.
(1 mark)

Q7　**36** and **81** *(1 mark)*

Q8　**The rule is: divide each number in the sequence by 3 to find the next number in the sequence.**
(1 mark)

Pages 64-65
— Number Patterns 2

Q1　**22** *(1 mark)*

Q2　**32**, **64** and **128** *(1 mark)*

Q3　**22** *(1 mark)*

Q4

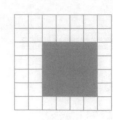

(1 mark)
There will be **49** shaded squares in the seventh shape.
(1 mark)
Because the sequence is made up of the square numbers increasing in size. The seventh square number is $7^2 = 49$.
(1 mark)

Q5　$187 - 5 = 182$
$182 \div 2 = \textbf{91}$
(2 marks — 1 mark for trying to subtract 5 and divide by 2, 1 mark for the correct answer.)

Q6　$17.2 - 2.4 = 14.8$
$14.8 \div 4 = 3.7.$
So ⭐ = **3.7**
(2 marks for correct answer and working. Otherwise 1 mark for attempt at working with one error.)
So the missing numbers are:
6.1, **9.8** and **13.5** *(1 mark)*

Q7　30🔪 + 30🍴 *(1 mark)*

Answers

Q1 **435** _(1 mark)_

Q2 **64** _(1 mark)_

Q3 **100** _(1 mark)_

Q4

Shape	Faces	Vertices
Cube	6	8
Triangular prism	5	6
Square-based pyramid	5	5

(2 marks for all correct answers. Otherwise 1 mark for 2 correct answers.)

Q5 **128** and **512** _(1 mark)_
Each new number in the sequence is four times the previous number. _(1 mark)_

Q6 E.g.

(1 mark for any rectangle covering 12 squares.)

Q7 The total number of boxes:
5 + 4 + 7 = 16
Total number of packets:
16 × 36 = 576
(2 marks for correct answer. Otherwise 1 mark for attempt to add up the number of boxes and multiply the total by 36.)

Q8 **35°** _(1 mark)_

Q9 **6** more salami pizzas were sold on Saturday. _(1 mark)_
18 ham pizzas were sold on Friday. _(1 mark)_

Q10 Any one of **32**, **52** or **92**. _(1 mark)_
25 is a square number. _(1 mark)_

Q11 **40%** _(1 mark)_

Q12 **128°** _(1 mark — allow 127° to 129°)_

Q13 **787 m** _(1 mark)_
He will be 128 m from the playground, but only 102 m from the café.
He will be closest to the **café**. _(1 mark)_

Q14

(1 mark)

Q1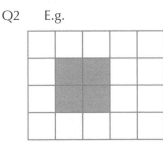

146.8 _(1 mark)_

Q2 E.g.

(Any 4 squares shaded for 1 mark.)

Q3 $9.4 - 7.8 = 1.6$
$1.6 \div 4 = 0.4$

⬡ $= 0.4$

(2 marks for the correct answer. Otherwise 1 mark for subtracting 7.8 from 9.4.)

Q4
$$6 \overline{)\ 2\ 0^24}$$
with quotient **3 4**

34 _(1 mark)_

Q5 $21 + 12 = 33$
$33 \div 3 = \mathbf{11}$ _(1 mark)_

Q6 **(3, 10)** _(1 mark)_

Q7 These numbers should be written on the spinner:

The positions of the numbers are not important. _(1 mark)_

Answers

Q8   **2.5 cm**, **50 mm**, **35 cm**, **0.5 m** *(1 mark)*

Q9   9 × 4 = **36 cm** *(1 mark)*

Q10

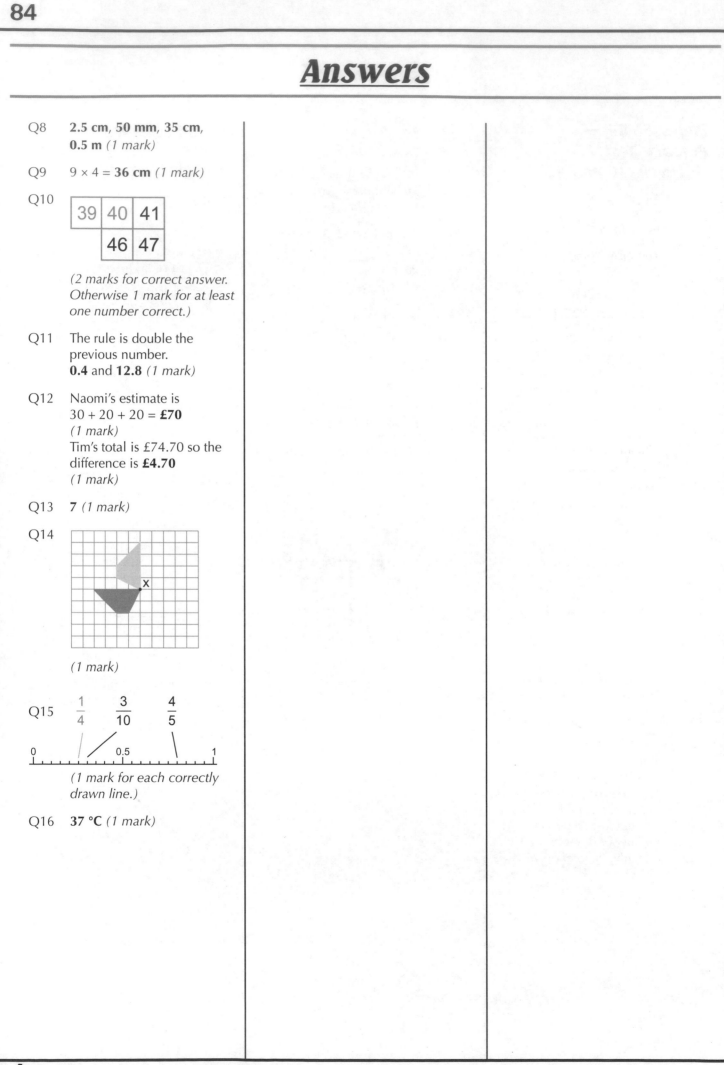

39	40	41
	46	47

(2 marks for correct answer. Otherwise 1 mark for at least one number correct.)

Q11   The rule is double the previous number.
0.4 and **12.8** *(1 mark)*

Q12   Naomi's estimate is
30 + 20 + 20 = **£70**
(1 mark)
Tim's total is £74.70 so the difference is **£4.70**
(1 mark)

Q13   **7** *(1 mark)*

Q14

(1 mark)

Q15 $\frac{1}{4}$ $\frac{3}{10}$ $\frac{4}{5}$

(1 mark for each correctly drawn line.)

Q16   **37 °C** *(1 mark)*